Redneck Woman

GRETCHEN WILSON

with Allen Rucker

Redneck Woman

STORIES FROM MY LIFE

WARNER BOOKS

NEW YORK   BOSTON

Complete permissions for lyrics reprinted in this book may be found on pages 201–202.

Warner Books

Hachette Book Group USA

1271 Avenue of the Americas

New York, NY 10020

Visit our Web site at www.HachetteBookGroupUSA.com.

Printed in the United States of America

First Edition: November 2006

10 9 8 7 6 5 4 3 2 1

Warner Books and the "W" logo are trademarks of Time Warner Inc. or an affiliated company. Used under license by Hachette Book Group USA, which is not affiliated with Time Warner Inc.

Library of Congress Cataloging-in-Publication Data

Wilson, Gretchen, 1973–
   Redneck woman : stories from my life/Gretchen Wilson with
   Allen Rucker. —1st ed.
         p. cm.
   Summary: Country music personality Gretchen Wilson offers up her rags-to-riches tale with the same storytelling that fuels her songwriting and inspires millions of fans to both celebrate and identify with this self-styled Redneck Woman.
   ISBN-13: 978-0-446-58001-4
   ISBN-10: 0-446-58001-5
1. Wilson, Gretchen, 1973–   2. Country musicians—Biography.
I. Rucker, Allen.   II. Title.
ML420.W5528G74 2006
782.421642092—dc22
[B]   2006021645

Cover credits: *Hair and makeup: Candy Burton*
                Stylist: Christiev Alphin

This book is dedicated
to my daughter,
Grace…
You are my reason

CONTENTS

ACKNOWLEDGMENTS

I have not only been blessed with the life I've been given but also by the wonderful people who surround me and helped make this book possible. They include all the folks we interviewed for the book: my family, Big O, and Big and Rich. Also, David Haskell, Michele Schweitzer, Crystal Dishmon, Dennis Willis, Jess Rosen, Tanya Welch and Tracy Fleaner at Sony, Mel Berger and Greg Oswald at William Morris, my co-writer Allen Rucker, and my editor at Warner Books, Colin Fox.

A special thanks to a few people for giving me some of the greatest advice a new girl can get: John Grady, Connie Bradley, Donna Hilley, Anthony Martin, Sue Leonard, my booking agent Barbara Hardin, and my managers Marc Oswald and Dale Morris.

And last, but not least, one more hug for my precious Grace, who has taught me what it means to truly live. You are my inspiration.

INTRODUCTION

Swinging doors and cleaning floors is all I'd ever
  known
and out of nowhere somehow I found my yellow
  brick road
so when you're broke and paying dues,
look at me I'm living proof
and if there's hope for me
I know there's hope for you

"Not Bad for a Bartender"

It was my ninth showcase, I think, my ninth time to go in front of a Nashville record company executive, sing a few songs, and try to walk away with a record deal. The first eight tryouts had been stone-cold rejections, for a hundred reasons. I didn't have the right look. My hair was dated. I didn't have the beauty-queen bone structure of many of the female stars currently topping the charts. I was a little too old, a little too heavy, a little too hard-edged, a little too rock and roll, a little too something. Rumor had it that I occasionally chewed tobacco and enjoyed a shot of Jack Daniel's. My friend Big Kenny thinks that a lot of those deal-making executives, used to new talent that they could dress, mold, and manipulate, took one look at me and said to themselves,

"There's no way in hell I can control *that* woman." Well, at least on one count, they were dead right.

So the night before this particular showcase—scheduled to take place in the office of the then president of Sony Music Nashville, John Grady—I found out that the appointment was for eight the next morning. I started freaking out. I called my new manager, Dale Morris, and said, "Dale, eight o'clock in the morning is way too early to sing. I can't do that. I'm a bartender. I'm a club singer. I've been singing from nine P.M. to two A.M. my whole life!"

Dale said, "Well, then, get up at six."

I said, "What?"

He said, "Get up at six and it won't seem so darn early. Eight A.M. will seem like ten A.M. and you can sing your heart out."

And that's what I did. That morning, waiting to go into that office and sing to a man behind a desk, I was so scared. Doing an in-office musical showcase is always an unsettling experience. You feel so naked standing there, often staring at a lineup of businessmen, and then having to pick a guitar and sing without a microphone, lights, loud amps, or anything else to boost your performance. It's so hard for someone who's creative to stand and let someone who's not creative judge them and tell them whether or not they are worthy of a commercial career. But, in this business, I'd come to realize, it's just something you have to do, and I had pretty well made up my mind that I wasn't going to turn tail and quit until they dragged me out of the last room of the last audition.

There was something about this moment that was oddly reminiscent of the very first time I had ever been paid to sing. I was all of fifteen and equally on edge. The venue, so to speak, was a little place called the Hickory Daiquiri Dock Bar and Grill in Collinsville, Illinois, a shotgun bar in a nondescript strip mall. My "act," never before tested in public, was to sing some much beloved country standards to the unamplified backup of music-only tapes on a portable tape recorder, kind of a homemade, do-it-yourself karaoke machine. I sat on the top of the bar in a blue evening gown and curled-up hair and sang for the Happy Hour crowd at the Dock. I was so scared that first time that I threw up for an hour before going on "stage," but I did it anyway. I knew I could sing.

I also knew I could sing when I walked into John Grady's office at eight that morning twelve years later but that was no guarantee that he would agree with me. I felt a little better this time because I had Dale Morris, one of the most powerful managers in Nashville, at my side. I also had Big Kenny and John Rich, then virtual unknowns, playing backup for me. They were people I loved and trusted, two of the soon-to-be-legendary "Godfathers" of the Muzik Mafia, the loose collection of eccentric Nashville singer-songwriters I had hooked up with. Dale Morris said that my only job that morning was to go in, shake hands, sing like it was eleven o'clock at night, and leave. He would take care of any business afterward, should there be any interest from the star-makers across the room.

So I walked in, smiled, shook a few hands, stood there, and started singing. I sang three songs, none of which I had written myself. I was in the middle of a passionate ballad, "Holdin' You," which later appeared on my first record, when I glanced up at the only person I was really singing for, John Grady, sitting behind his big desk. He didn't appear all that interested in my performance. In fact, he wasn't even looking at me. He seemed to be totally distracted, going through his desk drawers, looking for something to write with, like he needed to jot down a grocery list for the trip home that night. It was all very awkward, even more awkward than most in-office, let's-see-what-you-can-do-kid type auditions. I was trying to keep my cool and not glare back into his eyes, as if to say, nonverbally, "why, you inconsiderate prick." At the same time I was trying to sing a tender love song—". . . I feel like I'm falling apart, holding you holds me together . . ."— with some emotion at eight o'clock in the damn morning.

About halfway through the song, I noticed Mr. Grady start to write something on a piece of paper. From my vantage point, I could clearly see him write the letter "n" followed by the letter "o". As in . . . "NO." That was it, I thought. He's passing on me halfway through my three-song set and it looks like he had to write a note to remind himself. He folded the paper up and left it lying there on his desk while I went on to my third and last song. I couldn't wait to get out of that room.

As we said our goodbyes and headed out the door, I turned to Big Kenny and John and indicated that I was sure the guy hated me and was passing on me; after all, I had seen him writing "NO" right in front of me. About that time, John Grady tapped me on the shoulder, handed me the folded piece of paper, and said, "Here, I want you to have this." About halfway down the hall, hands shaking, I finally got up the courage to open that note.

It read, "NOW."

With that one word, the dream I had had since the age of seven started to come true.

I am a redneck woman, and proud to say so. I grew up in rural Illinois, the first child of a single mom who struggled to keep her life, and my life, on track. I grew up living in rental housing of one sort or another: trailers, apartments, tacky little houses, even a camper or two. I dropped out of school at age fifteen and pretty much supported myself as a waitress, bartender, and club and dive singer until I moved to Nashville at age twenty-three. For my first five years in Nashville, until I finally got the break that changed my life, I continued to tend bar, sing for anyone who would listen, and had a baby out of wedlock along the way.

Except for the fact that I got this extraordinary opportunity to write songs and sing about the people I grew up with and feel a deep love and admiration for, I am no different from them. Like them, I'm "just a product of my raising" and I still say "hey y'all" and "yee-haw."

In many parts of this country, "redneck" is an acceptable slur, along with equally acceptable put-downs like "white trash," "trailer trash," and "hillbilly." Low-income rural whites are about the last people in America who seem to be fair game for blatant stereotyping. Even media personalities who should know better regularly refer to Britney Spears as a white-trash queen or a NASCAR fan as a (dumb) redneck whose idea of entertainment is watching a bunch of stock cars going around in circles for hours. NASCAR, not to mention Britney Spears, are of course enormously popular and profitable, so the slurs are not as loud or frequent as they once were, but the attitude is still there. Say the word "redneck" or "trailer trash" in polite company outside of the South and everyone in the room will understand what you're getting at.

Like I, or any self-respecting redneck, could give a good rat's ass. We are way past the day where we automatically feel bad because we happen to live in the country, call a trailer our home, or get our hands dirty when we work a wage job. We have an ever-increasing sense of pride in who we are and where we come from, and some of this pride is starting to get noticed. Since I stopped doing work like waitressing and bartending and became known as a singer-songwriter, I have been asked the same question over and over again, whether I was in Stockholm, Sweden, Sydney, Australia, or Darlington, South Carolina. Everyone wants to know what I think it means, in a positive and truthful way, to be a Redneck Woman. I have always had to try and answer that question with one or two short sound bites and it's always been frustrating. It's too big a question to answer in a two-minute radio interview.

Since the redneck stereotype still exists in many places, and carries with it some pretty ugly associations of backwardness and racism, I thought this book might be the perfect opportunity to answer that often asked question—What does it mean to be a Redneck Woman?—and to describe in detail what the life of at least one such woman has been like.

As you will see, many of the most important—and powerful—people in my life are women: my incredible grandmother, my Aunt Vickie, my daughter, Grace, my mother, and the women of country music who inspired me from as far back as I can remember. This includes all the tough, resourceful, hardworking women I grew up around, the women I write about and sing about; none of them are "high-class broads." In many ways, this book is for women, especially women who find themselves in difficult or unglamorous circumstances. Despite the hardships, many such women love their life, have a great time being who they are, and shouldn't be told, by Hollywood or anyone else, that they should aspire to be something that they're not. On the other hand, for those women who feel stuck with the wrong job, the wrong husband, or a life they don't want, I can only repeat over and over again something I learned from my own life: If there is hope for me, there is hope for you.

Many of you already know what I'm talking about, of course, because you live it every day. To the rest of you, men and women, city or country, I say: Welcome to our world.

Now "let me get a big 'hell yeah' from the redneck girls like me . . ."

"Hell yeah!"

Again . . .

"Hell yeah!!!"

Redneck Woman

CHAPTER

POCAHONTAS PROUD

I'm the biggest thing that ever came from my hometown
And I'll be damned if I'm gonna let'em down
If it's the last thing I do before they lay me in the ground
You know I'm gonna make Pocahontas proud.

"Pocahontas Proud"

I grew up in the southern part of Illinois, a kind of no-man's-land between St. Louis on the west and the Indiana border on the east. The land is flat, as flat as Iowa or western Kansas. The horizon is broken by an occasional silo or water tower but otherwise is endless. There are plenty of cornfields and dairy farms, interrupted by small town after small town with names like Pierron, Dudleyville, Greenville, Edwardsville, Millersburg, and Pocahontas. Some of these towns are so small that their inhabitants just say they're from a particular county, like Bond County or Madison County. Pocahontas doesn't even have a grocery store. Pierron doesn't have a gas station or stoplight. I guess the four hundred people or so who live there don't need to stop that much.

Travelers whiz by on Interstate 70 from St. Louis to Indianapolis and rarely stop and investigate the places or the people who live within a stone's throw of that highway. A common saying is, no one comes to Pocahontas who doesn't already live there. It's part of a rural society that looks inward to the lives of its neighbors and not outward to the life of the world.

Although Illinois fought for the North in the Civil War, the area of Illinois that I'm from feels a lot more like the South. The region is very close in distance to Southern strongholds like Kentucky and Tennessee, much closer than it is to Chicago and the upper Midwest. The speech is Southern—people say "carn" for corn, "fark" for fork, and "arwl" for oil. The name of the Interstate is Highway "Farty," not Forty. More importantly, the outlook is more Southern than Northern. The people there feel a part of the great traditional Southern culture that has now made huge inroads into every part of America—country music, stock car racing, pickup trucks, and Jack Daniel's whiskey. If you think about it, the South really did rise again, and is still rising, in ways no one could have predicted.

My mom, Christine, gave birth to her only daughter, Gretchen Frances Wilson, when she was sixteen. My father, who I didn't really meet until I was twelve years old, was a local boy she had married at fifteen. Her main reason for marriage, she says, was to get out of her childhood household and escape from a tyrannical father. She dropped out of school in the beginning of the tenth grade and now claims she didn't have much time for school even when she went because of the demands her father put on her—everything from baby-sitting her younger brother, Vern, to moving rock piles for one of her dad's many landscaping projects. She soon tired of her new husband (my father) because, even as a teenager, she was forced to work two jobs—waitressing and housecleaning—while he was struggling to find one.

She left my biological father after two years and soon met up with her second husband, my stepfather, who to this day she rightly refers to as "the dark one." At the time of their marriage, my mom was eighteen and he was twenty-eight. He was a smooth operator, the kind of charmer who could talk anyone into anything. He talked my beautiful, blond, adventurous teenage mom into marriage and made her life—and much of my life—a living hell for the next sixteen years.

My mom married my stepfather for stability and he was anything but stable. He made his living as an itinerant, self-employed contractor and builder—anything from bricklaying to deck-building—and he knew a hundred ways to often talk people out of their money. He would bid a job, for instance, take half the money up front for materials, buy half the materials, do half the work, and then just take off with the rest of the money. And he'd often do this to people who didn't have the where-withal to find him. There were always a lot of angry people looking for him.

In my mom's words, he was a master at "playing the role." One way or another, he was always making money but he could waste it on pursuing the next job as fast as he made it. At the end of the day, he never had anything to show for it.

Soon after her second marriage, my mom had another child, my stepbrother, half-brother, Josh, who I now just call my brother since we've been so close for so long. Because of my stepfather's methods of doing business, we were always moving. My stepfather would be ready to walk away from a job half-done or maybe the rent became due on the trailer or apartment we were living in at the moment, and it would be pack-up-and-get-out time. My mom would pack Josh and me, along with the dog and cat and a few meager belongings, into her beat-up Ford Escort and away we would go. Sometimes we'd only go ten miles, from one little town to another, rent another trailer with nothing more than my stepfather's solemn promise to pay the rent after he got his first paycheck from a job he only claimed to have.

So we were always moving on, always running from debt, never having enough money to stop, plant roots, and live a normal life. I spent a large part of my childhood on the move, never really sure which unfurnished rental unit to call home. Moving was our principal family activity. We moved an average of every three or four months from the time my mom met the dark one until the time I took off on my own at age fifteen. I'm from Pocahontas, but I have lived in some form of temporary residence in Collinsville, Edwardsville, Belleville, Troy, St. Jacob, Greenville, Millersburg, Pierron, and Glen Carbon, all towns in the same general area. Consequently I kept switching school districts every time we moved. Even within one school year, I might find myself as the new kid in class in three or four different elementary or junior high schools. I probably attended twenty different schools from the time I began kindergarten until I finally quit in the beginning of the ninth grade. For both Josh and me, it was an endlessly crazy existence.

Life in rural Illinois is tough even if you're not moving every five minutes and running scams to stay alive. Everybody there struggles. Outside of farming, which is one of the hardest lives imaginable, there isn't much around there that could pass for a local economy. The best you can hope for, if you don't feel tied to the place and the people, is to latch on to some kind of skill or career that can take you out of there.

If you stay, your options are damn few. You're going to be a pig farmer or a corn farmer, or you're down at a diner or truck stop flipping eggs, or you're an auto mechanic working in a small shop in your backyard, or a hod-carrier, or you're pouring drinks down at Hoosier Daddy's. At least while I was growing up, everyone was pretty much in the same boat—barely making it and trying to deal with all the side effects of barely making it, like alcohol, divorce, and despair.

Like in most people's lives, there were good times and there were bad times. During the good times, when work was plentiful and the cash was flowing, we might move into a nice-sized house and feel almost like the people we'd see in the TV commercials serving Pillsbury biscuits in the kitchen or washing the new car in the driveway. During the bad times, I felt more like the homeless people you see on the six o'clock news. I remember, between houses or trailers, sleeping in the back of a pickup truck, more than once. The truck would have a camper shell on the back and we'd crawl into sleeping bags and call it a night. During those hard times, though, I never felt like a victim. I felt like a survivor. I knew things would change—they always did—and I was just anxious to keep moving and maybe find a place, for whatever length of time, where I could take a deep breath and try to enjoy where I was.

One day when I was about six, my mother's husband decided that he wanted to move to Miami, Florida. He had an uncle down there who could line him up with some prospects and, according to my mom, he saw it as a way to get away from all our in-laws in Southern Illinois so my mother wouldn't have anyone to run to when things got rough. In Miami, we were completely surrounded by strangers, often strangers who couldn't speak English, and completely dependent on my stepfather for guidance and protection. Which is exactly how he liked it.

Even in southern Florida, we never sat still for long. In the five or six times we relocated there, we lived in South Miami, North Miami, and Coral Gables, among other scenic stops. Not only did we impulsively move from Greenville, Illinois, to Dade County, Florida, when things got tough, we'd often live in three different places in Florida in a six- or seven-month period. It was a way of life.

I could see why my mother wanted to live in Miami— she was still very young and wanted the wild Miami lifestyle of the 1980s. To Josh and me, it was pure culture shock. We didn't move to postcard Miami; we moved to trailer-park Miami, a far different world than the one of the South Beach partygoers celebrated on *Entertainment Tonight.* We often lived down there among the lowest-income Cuban refugees you could find. At one point, our next-door neighbor was an old Cuban gentleman named Flaco. Flaco and his wife were in their seventies and kind of took Josh and me under their wing, for a little while anyway. They had a pet parrot that spoke Spanish. They were kind of a substitute for the grandparents we had left behind in Illinois.

The trailer park where we and Flaco lived was a big one—maybe four-hundred trailers in one enclosed area. It was way, way out of Miami, almost in the Everglades. It's where civilization ended. Our rent-a-trailer was small—twelve by sixty—and housed four of us. It had a screened-off porch where Josh and I played Nintendo by the hour and even played pool on a pint-sized pool table. The pool cue would always be hitting a wall, making it impossible to really shoot, but we did it anyway.

Flaco made his living by selling roses on the street. His trailer was only a bush line away from a big intersection, so he would simply hop over his fence every day, grab a bucket of roses from his wife, and peddle them to the cars stopped at the red light. Even at his age, he stood out there in that traffic for hours on end. Again, this wasn't fun-loving Miami. Flaco rarely hung out at the beach and neither did I. In the on-and-off four or five years we lived in South Florida, I bet I can count on one hand the number of times I went to the beach.

Miami and Southern Illinois were two completely different worlds, like living on Earth one day and Mars the next. And making the transition back and forth was always weird. I'd go from hanging out with a bunch of Spanish-speaking motor-cycle friends at Lowman's Plaza in Miami at twelve or thirteen to sitting under the bleachers at a high school football game in Illinois with some fresh-faced country boy trying to get to first base. The boy in the bleachers had never been anywhere as far as one county over and had a curfew. The guys in Miami were adept at surviving in all kinds of worlds, Cuban and American, and didn't know what a curfew was—they couldn't even pro-nounce the word. In fact, they couldn't even say my name. They called me "G."

I had no choice but try to fit in as best I could in both worlds. I learned enough Spanish so that I could understand my math teacher; her English was so bad that teaching in Spanish made more sense. Even today, I know enough Spanish that if I'm in a restaurant and some guys are talking trash in the next booth in Spanish, I can understand them and lip off to them in their own language. They always freak out.

Shifting back and forth between these places was always disorienting and often painful. It was very hard trying to grow up and come into your adolescence not knowing where the hell you were, let alone who the hell you were. Looking back, I can now see that the experience of living in Florida may have opened me up in ways that a more grounded exis-tence in rural Illinois wouldn't have. It gave me both a famil-iarity and a curiosity about the rest of the world, maybe even a taste for the new and exotic.

Many people growing up in small-town Midwestern America have no real sense of the world beyond their imme-diate surroundings. They are often fearful of the larger world and figure that if they ventured out, they'd be like the proverbial rube in the big city—scared, gullible, and an easy mark. At the very least, they think, they'll get robbed and beaten for just walking down the wrong street. The city, any city, is foreign territory.

I learned early in life that the big city was often strange and different, but no more intimidating than downtown Pocahontas on a Saturday night. Both Josh and I often had to fend for ourselves in the urban environment of Miami while our parents were having a good time or plotting the next move. And as with all the other obstacles that were thrown in our path as kids, we survived just fine.

No matter where we were—Illinois or Florida—our family life was a constant merry-go-round of feast and famine. In Florida, for instance, with my mom working full-time at Tony Roma's and her husband hitting a good streak in the deck- or dock-building business, we'd have a little spending cash. In a gesture of living large and probably stroking his own ego, my stepfather would go out and buy my mom a brand-new used car for her birthday. Two weeks later he'd have to sell the same car to pay the rent or to underwrite our next move out of the area. Perhaps that car would finance our way back to Illinois and another town, another trailer, and another short-term job to keep food on the table.

People often think kids don't see the stress and anxiety in their parents' lives or even if they do see it, can just roll with it and not be affected. In my experience, that is nonsense. Josh and I picked up on everything. We were smart enough to see that our school friends didn't live like this, assuming

9

we made any school friends in the three or four months we spent at any one school. We knew that it was weird to suddenly move into an apartment or trailer on the first of the month and be out of there before the next rent check was due. We knew that when my mom announced that we were off to Miami again and followed it with "we're going to stay in one place and your dad's got a great new job and this time it's going to be different"—we knew it wasn't going to be a bit different. After a while, of course, we'd pack up and leave with my mom making no such promises of a new life right around the next corner. She realized we weren't buying that line of BS after hearing it a dozen times. We all knew the truth: that life was a damn mess all the time.

And most of all, we could see and feel the abuse. My stepfather was never a big drinker, a drug user, or even a cigarette smoker, but he was often violent and abusive, especially toward my mother. My mom lived in fear from the moment she married the man. The verbal abuse never stopped and the physical abuse was always one sassy comeback away. As she sees it now, my mom describes her whole existence as like being in an embryo position—curled up and cowering. For most of those sixteen years she saw herself as weak and powerless. He had her in a psychological prison.

Mom, only in her early twenties when the abuse became constant, didn't know what to do. As she's said many times, she was too scared to get out of this awful situation. Especially after moving to Miami, she was completely alone in fending off his attacks as well as trying to shield her two children from his wrath. She did call the police a few times when she felt her life was in jeopardy, but then was too scared to press charges or use the incident to get as far away from him as possible. The police themselves would bring him up on assault-and-battery and he would do time in the county jail, but the sentences never lasted that long and when he got out, my mom would be there to take him back in.

This kind of relationship is an ugly, unbroken cycle of intimidation and compromise and only the people who have lived through it can understand it. And of course, ours wasn't the only household in America where this cycle is a simple fact of daily life. All you have to do is tune into Oprah or Dr. Phil to know the widespread reach of domestic abuse in America.

My mom did try to escape this torment five or six times in their long marriage. On occasion, she would put Josh and me in the car in Miami and head back home for the love and support of her family. But he was always one step ahead of her. Before she got back to Pocahontas, he would have taken a flight from Miami and be there to greet her at the door. Then he would use his vast storehouse of charm and BS to lure her back, all the time telling her the same lie she was constantly telling us, i.e., "this time it'll be different."

Or, if that didn't work, he'd resort to pure intimidation. He'd tell her straight out that if she didn't come back, he was going to kill her, her two kids, her mom and dad, and any other jackass who dared to step in and tell him how to treat his wife or live his life. And she believed him. She had no doubt that he had the capacity to eliminate anyone who got in his way.

My mom tried to show us a normal childhood amidst all this craziness and fear. In Illinois, she signed us up for Little League baseball and kept us close to the loving influence of my blood relatives. In Miami, she kept me busy doing kid things. At times I felt like I was off to a different after-school activity every day of the week—Monday, ballet lessons; Tuesday, gymnastics; Wednesday, tap; and so on. I'll never forget this dance studio in Miami run by this Cuban woman named Miss Jerry. My only English-speaking friend there at the time, Amber, and I were all of five years old and scared to death of Miss Jerry. She would never harm us, but she was strong and assertive in a way that I rarely saw other women, especially my mom. She definitely left an impression.

Throughout all the confusion of growing up on the move, my saving grace, then as now, was my family. When we were located anywhere in Southern Illinois, I spent a lot of time with my grandparents, my Uncle Vern, only six years older, and my Aunt Vickie. They were my escape from the tension of living with my mom and even though their lives were occasionally pretty nuts, they seemed normal and stable compared to mine. I did things with them that remain some of the fondest memories of my childhood, whether picking wild berries with my grandma in the woods behind her trailer or learning to ride a motorbike with Uncle Vern. It didn't take a village to raise me, but it took the love of my extended family to help me survive and grow.

When I was twelve, for instance, we were living in Miami and my mom thought I was running a little too wild with the urban kids I hung with. She was also having a particularly tough time with her husband and trying to leave him for the third or fourth time. So she packed me up and sent me back to Pocahontas, or Pokey, for the summer to live with my Aunt Vickie and her then husband, Eric Simmonds.

My Aunt Vickie was, and still is, a hard worker. For a lot of her adult life, she was a welder. She welded airplane parts at a sub-factory in St. Louis for use in military planes made by McDonnell Douglas in the same area. She drove to St. Louis every workday for twenty years. Depending on the exact location of her home at the time, it was an hour or so in and an hour or so back. Both she and Eric got up at 4:30 every morning to make the long trek into the city. She spent half her time welding steel and half her timing applying spray paint. She's probably filled her lungs with plenty of noxious fumes.

So I went to live with Aunt Vickie that summer and what a great summer it was! Vickie and Eric lived in a double-wide trailer at the time and had a couple of kids. My job was to watch the kids during the day and have fun the rest of the time. A lot of that fun revolved around Eric's major passion in life—racing stock cars.

Saturday nights in the summertime was racing season around there. There was a quarter-mile, all-dirt track in Highland, a much bigger town than Pokey, and a huge crowd would gather there every Saturday night to drink, fight, drink some more, and watch their local favorites speed around in the dirt. Eric drove street stock—cars called "bombers"—which was the down-and-dirty class at the Highland Racetrack. He had one old Chevy that he raced and a garage bigger than his home to work on it. The car looked like crap but the engine was a masterpiece. When he wasn't working or racing, he was out in that garage working on his car. If half the men in the area on any given night were knocking back a can of Busch in a local tavern, the other half were in some buddy's garage, knocking back a can of Busch and arguing about carburetors and spark plugs.

The races were a trip. You'd drive over to the track at Highland and sit in a great big tin-covered bleacher seat with chicken-wire fencing separating you from the track. For most people, it was like a big outdoor party every Saturday night, an excuse to get sloshed with their friends, cheer on their next-door neighbor, and forget about all the problems waiting back home. The drunk and disorderly would slip and fall into each other's laps or spill beer down the back of each other's shirt. The whole arena was one big mosh pit.

And the fights were worth the price of admission alone. Especially in the bomber class, there was a crash on almost every spin and every crash would foment an argument in the stands. The worst offenders tended to be the wives of the race drivers themselves, women like my Aunt Vickie. Wife #1 would say something about her husband getting rear-ended by someone else's husband—"Why that dumb-ass SOB just ran into my husband!"—and wife #2 would leap over fifteen people to beat the crap out of #1. The stock car wives were a breed apart. I always thought there was a great movie about the wild lives of small-town stock car wives—along the lines of that movie about the murdering moms of Texas high school cheerleaders. These ladies of the track were a tough bunch of broads.

One photograph I still have and cherish sums up the sheer fun of going to those races for me. It's a picture of Vickie and Eric's son, Matt, my cousin, who today is still close by as one of the people working on my farm in Tennessee. Vickie, Matt, and I are in the stands at the races, watching Eric race his beat-up Chevy. Matt, all of eighteen months old, is sitting on his mom's lap. He's got on a hippie wig, is wearing earplugs to mute the tremendous noise of the cars, dressed in a diaper, and sporting an unlit cigarette in his mouth. At that moment, we were all in the Southern Illinois version of hillbilly heaven.

Along with watching others race around a track, I first learned to drive a truck that summer in Pocahontas. And an even bigger milestone took place—I drank my first beer.

One night Eric took off with his stock car buddies to drink and act up and he left Aunt Vickie home with me. Vickie was mad as hell. As the two of us sat around the kitchen table, cussing out Eric, I decided to light up a cigarette, a habit I had recently picked up from my Cuban pals in Miami. Vickie, at that point a nonsmoker, was shocked. "A cigarette? You're only twelve!" I told her I'd teach her how to smoke a cigarette if she would let me have a beer. She was just in the right mood to say yes. We then proceeded to go out to Eric's shed, steal his cooler of Busch, drink every last one of them, and stack the empties in a pyramid on the table for him to see. Although I didn't feel too good the next morning from all the beer and cigarettes, the whole experience was a whole lot of fun and something Vickie and I laugh about to this day.

How did my mom handle such a long-term abusive relationship? Unable, like many abused women, to walk away, she tried every way she could to block it out and numb herself from the fear and violence. She started working all night in a bar in Miami while her husband was between jobs. Before long she was hooked on cocaine and drinking heavily, addictions that weakened and tormented her for years. This only aggravated an already desperate situation and made her both more dependent on him and less able to take care of Josh and me. She was unhappy, depressed, and, in her own words, a broken person. And she pretty much remained this way until my stepfather was completely out of her life and she could finally see what a mess she had become.

The effect of all of this on me was pretty apparent: I had to develop a pretty thick skin—Vern likes to say that I became "bulletproof." What he means by this is that, at least in my dealings with the outside world, I grew a protective shield to ward off an attack, either emotional or physical. Like many women who grew up in circumstances like mine, I developed a wariness about who to trust and who not to trust. I didn't let someone get to know me or tell them anything personal until I was assured that they weren't going to take that information and turn it against me. I was the opposite of a sheltered, pampered child. I was never someone's little princess or "Daddy's little girl." Early on in life, I had what you might call a real hard edge.

Uncle Vern likes to tell stories about how he saw this in me when I was still a tomboy growing up in Pokey. Because we were only a few years apart in age—he was an afterthought, my grandma used to say—Vern was often my principal playmate—and tormentor. I used to shadow him constantly and he was always looking for ways to tease or test me. One of his favorite memories along this line happened when I was five or six. My grandpa grew hot peppers in the garden he had at the time. They were so hot that all you had to do was smell them and your eyes would start watering. So Vern saw me playing in the garden one day and figured it was time to introduce me to the world of tongue-burning peppers. He broke a pod in half and told me to stick it in my mouth. Which of course I did, because even at five, I was game for damn near anything.

His mom—my grandma—was washing dishes in the trailer and heard my bloodcurdling screams (I already had a strong voice). She came running out of the house with a wooden ladle and whacked Vern on the head for what seemed like forever. Vern claims that was the only time she ever laid a hand on him. All I know is that I never bite into a pepper today without thinking about how Vern introduced me to my first one.

Part of whatever bulletproofing I developed had to do with being raised in the country where kids had a lot of time to just screw around and had few places to do so. Vern's idea of a good time back then was to knock me down, get on top of me, pin me to the ground, work up a giant slimy hocker in his mouth, then get real close to my face, and proceed to shoot it right at me, then pull back at the very last second. Or he'd give me Indian burns until the skin would start to peel off my arm. Or, after he learned to ride a motorbike, he'd find his sweet little game-for-anything niece, stick me in a Radio Flyer wagon attached with a telephone cord to his 175 hp Kawasaki, and take off down a back country road going sixty miles an hour. Vern was a thrill-seeker and tried his best to turn me into one. I'd say he succeeded.

Also, Vern was a star athlete as a teenager. He played football and baseball in school at Greenville and was known by everyone who followed local sports. When he graduated from high school, he was offered a full scholarship from Southern Illinois University–Edwardsville to play baseball. His dad said, "Sorry, we ain't got enough money for gas," and that was that. For lack of gas money, Vern was denied a free college education. He got a job in the masonry business and started hauling bricks for a living.

A budding jock myself, I was always bugging him to play catch with me and as he got stronger and stronger, the pitches came faster and faster. By his mid-teens he was whizzing sixty- and seventy-mile fastballs at my head and though it scared the hell out of me, Vern claims I never walked away. I'd put the glove right in front of my face and take whatever he was throwing.

I don't think I would've had any of these experiences with testing my limits if I'd grown up in the suburbs. You can get toughened by economic stress or people around you who abuse or mistreat you, but you also toughen up by taking risks.

There is some connection, at least in my head, between taking that hot pepper from Vern and refusing to give up in the face of a lot of rejection when I got to Nashville. In both cases, you learn to take it and keep going.

Given the craziness surrounding me, I had to grow up fast. I had to walk into a new school in a new town every few months and devise a way to fit in and make the most of it. I had to fend off Cuban boys one day and whoop it up with good ol' boys the next. It takes an entirely different set of social skills to order lunch in those two worlds, let alone make friends and avoid enemies.

My first real boyfriend was an Italian man from Miami named Christopher Salvatore Leone. He ran a pool hall with his father on Byrd Road in South Miami. He was a cross between Rocky Balboa and Tony Danza—exotic, fun-loving, and tough. The relationship didn't last that long, but long enough to upset my grandpa. He especially hated Italians for some strange reason, maybe because they were Catholics or seemed to be having too good a time in life. My grandma, on the other hand, loved them all, even the New York mobster types. I, a crazy-ass hillbilly girl of thirteen or fourteen, had to figure it out all by myself. Without the guidance from an often spaced-out mother and a completely uncaring stepfather, I had to figure out how to handle many of the common problems of growing up. I also had to watch out for Josh, my little brother. And, given her state of helplessness and addiction, I often had to be the mother to my own mother.

The final episode in the sixteen-year-long saga of my mama and my hellish stepfather came after I had left home at fifteen and moved back to Illinois from Miami to live on my own. My mother and her husband had moved back soon after that, and my mom, in another fit of common sense, had separated from him again, hopefully for the last time. At the time she and Josh were living in Pocahontas with her parents, my grandma and grandpa, and Mom was tending bar at a tavern nearby. Her now estranged husband was living in a trailer in Collinsville, a few miles down the road.

As my mom tells the story, one afternoon he showed up at the bar where she was working and demanded that she accompany him back to his place in Collinsville. When she refused, he just pulled her into the car and took off. He drove to his trailer, threw her inside, and locked the doors. He had essentially kidnapped her and had no intention of letting her go until he vented his rage.

When I pulled up to the trailer, she came running out, panicked and completely naked for all the neighbors to see. She jumped in my car and we sped away from her irate husband. We immediately drove to the nearest hospital to have her examined. While we were sitting in the emergency room, her husband burst into the hospital and was ready to finish the job he had started in the trailer. Thank God hospital security and the police took over at this point, jumped him, and hauled him off to jail.

My mom went back to her parents' home to stay and my grandpa now had his shotgun cocked and ready in case the jerk decided to drop by and "patch things up" for the four hundredth time. Finally the court handed down a substantial sentence for terrorizing my mom—thirty-two days in the

Madison County jail. It wasn't nearly enough time to justify what he had done over so many years, but it was apparently sufficient for him to finally give up and leave us all alone. He never really bothered my mom again after that.

To this day, my brother, Josh, still finds a place in his heart for this man. Maybe Josh is the one person in the family he managed not to hurt.

I feel differently, of course. I feel like a large chunk of my childhood was damaged by that marriage. My mom shares some of the responsibility, of course. I think she did the best she could under some horrible circumstances. But, hey, I'm a redneck woman, remember, and I grew up a redneck girl. I'm "Pocahontas Proud," and as I say in that song, "You know, where I come from, we don't give up easily." I had plenty of strong people to help me keep going and not give up during my strange childhood, and the strongest of them all was my grandma.

2

THE ROCK

I knocked on every door on Music Row
But they looked down at me and said "Girl go back home"
You ain't got what we need in this town
But they couldn't whup the fighting side of me
You know, where I come from, we don't give up easily

"Pocahontas Proud"

The strongest, most dependable, most reliable people in my life have been women. I can't really explain it, but when I was growing up in rural Illinois, a lot of men were troubled, irresponsible, or in their own male world. They were often more of the problem than the solution. I'm no man-hater—far from it—but from a very early age I learned that if you ever expected a man to step in and make your life run more smoothly, you could be setting yourself up for a big heartache. In my experience, not only does a woman *not* need a man to

23

"complete" herself, she can often get much further along in life without one, or at least certain ones.

Where I came from, the women were simply a lot tougher and more resilient than most of the men. Many of the women would work at an outside job all day—everything from waitressing to farming to road-building—and then come home and do all of the cooking, all the housework, and all the child-rearing. The guys around there didn't know the first thing about washing a dish or adding bleach to a load of laundry. They'd do their own job all day, then come home and expect to be waited on by everyone else in the house. When I tended bar at Big O's Tavern in Pierron, Illinois, I'd see these women come by for a drink and maybe shoot some pool. By the time they got to the bar, they'd already put in two days' worth of work in one day and they were in no mood to put up with any crap from any guy in the place. One smart remark and they'd be ready to bash the guy's head in. Literally.

I continue to have a very high regard for the strong, resourceful women who choose this life of work and family and have the guts and determination to pull it off. There was one woman in particular who epitomized this self-sufficient streak. Her name was Diane Jackson. When I was young, my Uncle Vern and I would spend a lot of time down at Diane's house. She lived in a mobile home about a mile and a half down the road from our trailer. She and her husband, Jerry, an auto mechanic, had four or five boys and one girl, named Melissa. Vern and Jeff, one of her boys, were best friends and I just tagged along to start trouble. Even with all those kids,

Diane was always happy to see us. The family lived in two mobile homes sitting next to each other. They were welded together, I think, the back door of one leading right into the front door of the other. The kids lived in one of the homes and Diane and Jerry lived in the other one. And these weren't showroom trailers, either. They were beat up pretty badly.

Vern and I liked to go down there not only because of all the kids to play with, but also because they had an above-ground swimming pool behind their place. I don't know how in the hell they afforded that, but they did. None of us could afford air-conditioning, so on a hot summer day, we'd head to the Jackson pool. It was an absolute luxury.

Jerry Jackson was a little guy, probably around five feet six and weighed no more than a buck twenty. Diane was short but very heavy. And she was a dynamo. On any given day of the week, you'd walk into her house and the scene would be pretty much the same. Her youngest boy, probably three or four, would have a pacifier in his mouth and a diaper on his bottom and be hanging on Diane like a monkey. She had really short red hair that she kept in pigtails, wore no makeup, and would usually be dressed in nothing but a great big Cross Your Heart bra and a pair of spandex shorts. It was invariably hot in those trailers and Diane dressed for comfort.

So you'd walk in and there she'd be, dressed in her bra and shorts, wrangling kids and usually talking on the phone. She had a phone with an extra-long cord that could reach all over both trailers and she would lug the receiver around, yakking away, as she was doing fourteen other things. Her main activity was usually frying cheeseburgers. Twenty-four hours a day, seven days a week, it seemed, she'd be standing over a hot stove, frying cheeseburgers. She was feeding eight to ten people all the time, not to mention the likes of Vern and me dropping by at suppertime, and she was usually so busy that she didn't have time to dress, let alone sit down, have a cocktail, and watch the evening news.

Nobody's ever heard of Diane Jackson, but she was a huge part of my life and an inspiration to be around. She ran the whole show. That whole household would've fallen completely apart if she had gotten a cold or decided to take a day off. Two trailersful of people depended on her in every way and she assumed the responsibility like that's the way God intended things to be. She didn't really have time to question her life. She was too busy frying up a new batch of cheeseburgers.

Jerry was a good man, as far as I know, but like many of the men I grew up around, he was silent and withdrawn. They didn't talk much. They'd just do their job and come in at the end of the day full of grease and smelling like a workingman. They'd eat their supper, drink their two beers, and then go to bed, ready to get up the next morning and do the same thing all over again. You'd hardly hear anything out of them. They were just happy to be breathing. I'm not kidding. They were lucky that their wife didn't kill them in the middle of the night. And many were exceedingly lucky to have a wife like Diane who kept things together.

A lot of these strong, self-defined women were farmer's wives. My best friend in kindergarten was a girl named Nancy Gaffner and her parents ran a large-scale dairy farm.

Nancy was one of five or six kids and they lived in a ranch-style home with a big basement that seemed like a mansion to me at the time. Everyone worked on the farm, keeping the milk flowing, and Nancy's mom, Edith, a short, Susie-Homemaker-looking woman, worked like a dog to make sure the whole family stayed focused, healthy, and fed. All I saw her do every time I visited was cook and clean. Sounds boring, but it was absolutely critical to keeping the family enterprise going and she approached it like a mission. Three times a day the family would come in from the farm at a set time and a feast would await them. For breakfast, for instance, it was homemade biscuits and gravy and grits and bacon and eggs and sausage. The crew would come in, eat until they were full, and get back to the cows. They hardly spoke, including Edith. They were farm people. They didn't have time for idle chitchat. They had work to do.

What struck me about Edith, even as a little kid, was the high level of respect in which she was held by the rest of the family. She never had to ask anyone to take off their hat or clean up before sitting down to eat. She never had to ask anyone to remember to say grace. In her quiet, unassuming way, she demanded respect and she got it. Her authority didn't come from any external power. It came from inside, simply by the way she conducted herself. And as an example of dignity, she left a permanent impression on me.

My grandma, Frances Oneida Heuer, was the most solid person in our entire family. She was the rock, the stone.

Her husband, my grandfather Vernon, was, for a good part of his life, a one-legged alcoholic with a nasty outlook on things and a general dislike for humanity. He spent years engaged in the time-wasting practice of drinking from eight o'clock in the morning until eight o'clock every night, then griping and bitching at anyone within shouting distance, then going to bed.

My grandma had a mysterious past. Her maiden name, Storey, was given to her when she was adopted by a woman who ran a home for wayward girls in Peoria, Illinois. Grandma was an orphan. She never knew the identity of either her biological mother or father. Her birth certificate was made when she was ten years old, so even its authenticity is in doubt. Our whole family has done a fair amount of investigation into her origins and we never came up with any definitive answers. My grandmother's theory, which she believed in deeply, was that her adoptive mother's brother was her real father and that her real mother was a fourteen- or fifteen-year-old runaway who was staying in their home in Peoria at the time of her birth. Though there is no hard evidence to back this up, Grandma held on to this belief about her origins until the day she died.

My grandma kept her most valued keepsakes in a small jewelry box, a little wooden treasure chest with lion's heads on the front that I have held on to and cherished to this day. Among her meager possessions in that box were photos of her supposed father, whose name was Burt Wells, along with his death certificate and a newspaper clipping announcing his death. She felt her adoptive mother raised her out of guilt more than love. Her adoptive mother, she'd like to tell us, was hardly the nurturing maternal type. She was the kind of woman, Grandma would say, who would send you out after your own stick when you were about to get a beating. Apparently she carried a dog collar around her neck to whip my grandma when she acted up. It was a painful and confusing childhood.

Since none of us in the family know where my grandmother came from—including her ethnic background, her parents' country of origin, their way of life, and so on—we don't really know where we came from, either. It's as if our family tree began all over again with my grandmother. If you know nothing about your forebears, you are always a little unsure of your own identity. Maybe this is why I've always felt such a deep attachment to my roots in Southern Illinois and my closest blood relatives.

No matter her nationality, my grandma was a beautiful woman. She had jet black hair, hazel eyes, and very fair skin. To me, her adoring granddaughter, she looked like Snow White, a fairy princess. But her life was in many ways tragic. The love of her life, or so she told us, was a man who served in World War II and died shortly thereafter of leukemia. He was only twenty-three at the time. She loved him deeply, and for the rest of her life she kept every memory of him she could find—a folded American flag, probably the one that accompanied his funeral, was with her always, along with a few love letters and postcards that he sent her during their brief romance.

Shortly after this man's untimely death, my grandma started going out with and soon married my grandpa. Before long, she divorced him, married another man, had a baby, then divorced him, and remarried my grandpa. Later on, my Aunt Vickie did the same thing: marry a guy, divorce him, then marry him again. It's kind of a family tradition. For some reason, we all have trouble finding a good one!

In my grandma's case, the reason for sticking with my grandpa was understandable, in a sad sort of way. My grandpa was the brother of the love of her life, the man who died of leukemia. She married the closest person she could to the man she loved the most.

Unfortunately, love and marriage don't work like that. You usually don't fall in love with the next best thing. My grandparents never seemed particularly in love, at least to me; they didn't even seem particularly compatible. But their marriage stuck and together they had three children—my mother, Christine, my Aunt Vickie, and my Uncle Vern. (My grandma also had two babies die on her.) My Grandpa Vernon had injured his leg in the war, then crushed the same leg in a motorcycle accident a few years later. When gangrene set in, he had to have it amputated at the knee. He owned a prosthetic leg but for some reason, probably just orneriness, he refused to use it. He'd put an Ace bandage around his nub, fold his jeans up, tuck them in the back over his belt, and hobble around with a pair of crutches.

As I learned when I got older, my grandpa had had a terrible childhood. Born to a stern breed of Midwestern Germans, he was forced at ten years old, during the worst days of the Depression, to leave his parents and work on his grandparents' farm, doing mind-numbing, backbreaking labor for fourteen hours a day. On his deathbed, delusional with late-stage cancer, he'd call out, "Please, don't make me go back out there. It's too cold tonight. I've killed enough chickens." It was clearly a torturous existence.

He lied about his age and joined the Army at seventeen, and after the war worked for years as a Ford car mechanic, both before and after he lost his leg. After I learned to drive, he was always bugging me about my car. "When was the last time you checked that 'arwl'?" He had a lot of skills. Even with one leg, he was a master trap shooter. According to Vern, he could sit in a wheelchair and hit a hundred out of a hundred clay birds at sixteen yards any day of the week.

Then alcohol and bitterness took over. By the time I first got to know him, he hardly did anything all day but drink, cuss, and make everyone around him scared or miserable. Vern likes to say that because his dad was such a slave driver, he felt like he was in the Marines when he was ten. He also had a terrible temper. He'd get mad and start throwing anything he could find at Vern's head—one of his crutches, a pipe wrench, even a steel trash can if it was handy. My Aunt Vickie had her own strategy—lie low in the weeds and pay attention. She also got out of the house by eighteen. Grandpa was a tough old bird and I think some of that toughness rubbed off on all of us, including me.

My grandpa's nasty attitude was often directed toward anyone who wasn't like him. In fact, he was probably the most prejudiced, backward hillbilly I've ever met. And it really was just ignorance. He wasn't a particularly bad person, he was just deeply prejudiced. And it wasn't just toward blacks, either. Everyone, in his twisted view, was "a no-good rummy"—Irish, Hispanic, Japanese, Italian, Jewish, Catholic, people from New Jersey, it didn't really matter. He was an equal-opportunity bigot. If you didn't look or act like him, you were a second-class citizen in his eyes.

St. Louis, only about fifty miles away, was a foreign country to him, full of blacks and other suspect minorities who'd stab you in the back for a pack of cigarettes. As I said, many people in the small towns I grew up in felt that way towards St. Louis. They rarely ventured there for any reason. They watched the six o'clock news and only saw a city full of drug addicts, drive-by shootings, and marauding teenage gangstas. They never saw ordinary, hardworking, family people who just happened to be black.

My grandfather felt equally superior to women. Even though my grandma brought in most of the earned income in the family, he wouldn't let her get her driver's license, let alone drive "his" car, usually a late-model Ford or Ford truck. Driving was "man's work," I guess he figured, and about the only work he did for years was driving her back and forth from her paying job every day.

Despite Grandpa's less-than-winning personality, my grandma took care of him and put up with him for forty-five years of marriage. They lived pretty much their whole life in mobile homes and trailer parks and, as they got older, small, quiet trailer parks that catered to senior citizens. The home I remember best was an old trailer situated alone in the country on Rural Route 2 outside Greenville, Illinois. The first thing you saw when you drove up the gravel road was not the trailer, but my grandfather's big shed where he kept his tools and assorted junk. He rarely spent any time in their home. If he wasn't gone, he was holed up in his shed, doing God knows what.

Inside their trailer, besides the big TV that everybody watched, were always two things Grandpa Vernon cherished: a giant, stuffed hundred-pound swordfish he'd once caught on a fishing trip to Florida, and an old grandfather clock. The clock was a constant source of irritation for the old man, as if he needed something else to irritate him. He was always fiddling with it, trying to get it to work right. The fish and the clock—those were his heirlooms. Uncle Vern still has them to this day.

Grandpa had his favorite pastimes, and NASCAR was one of the biggest. Like all diehard NASCAR fans, he connected with certain drivers, Bill Elliott being number one in his mind for a good twenty years. Other than that, for most of my childhood, Grandpa's only "job" was to collect Social Security and disability from the government, and drink. He'd get up early, drive down to the VFW Hall in Greenville, and sit and drink with his veteran buddies all day. Meanwhile, my grandma worked like a dog to make ends meet. She worked forty, fifty hours a week for most of her life. Work paid the bills but it was also a way for her to escape from the madhouse of her personal life. For a long time she was a waitress at a place called the Round Table in Collinsville, Illinois. At one point, she even filled in at Big O's, the bar where both my mom and I worked for years. Like Diane Jackson, she ran the whole damn show.

I was just a little girl and from my perspective, it was a strange situation. My grandma and grandpa lived their whole life hating each other—I mean, truly hating each other—and yet he couldn't live without her, and she really had no interest in living without him. He didn't so much abuse her as ignore her, taking her efforts for granted and spending or hoarding money as he saw fit. As far as I can recall, she never got a birthday present or even a Christmas card from the old man, let alone a night out on their anniversary. He'd give her $40 at Christmastime to buy presents for everyone else in the family, but not herself. There's never been a present under the tree that read "From Vernon to his loving wife, Frances." Never.

They never even slept in the same room. In fact my grandma would pile stuff on her bed in her little bedroom and sleep every night on the couch in the living room. Grandpa would just go to his room, slam the door, and not be heard from again until morning. It's as if they had signed a lifelong pact to stick it out together, no matter their feelings. It was not a "modern" marriage.

I'm sure that there were times when my grandmother didn't know what kept her going. In moments of pure frustration, she'd yell, "Who in the hell else would put up with all this if I didn't?" She just figured she had to, I guess, and then didn't give it a second thought. She was stubborn and took pride in toughing it out. Her attitude was, "By God, I don't care what in the hell life hands me, I'll find a way to deal with it. I'll keep moving forward." That's the kind of thinking I got from her.

I mean, what else was she going to do? She had no father or mother or siblings to go home to. Grandpa and the rest of our little clan was all the family she had in the world. She didn't even know where she came from.

Though she could never make the decision to pack up and move away from the old man, it got to the point a time or two where Grandma made plans to bump him off and put both of them out of their misery. This was not some TV show; this was real life when a drastic situation called for drastic action. She later told me all about it. On one such occasion Grandma had the bright idea of sneaking into Vernon's room before he got home from the VFW and spraying down his bed with Lysol laced with some household poison. The plan was that he would slowly inhale the fumes, die a quiet respiratory death in his sleep, and no one, at least in and around Greenville, Illinois, would detect the cause. Of course he didn't die in his sleep. He just got up the next morning, coughed a little, cursed the world, and took off for another day of leisure.

On another occasion, she tried to kill him by putting motor oil in his soup. Just a touch, I guess, to make him deathly ill and keel over from a ruptured intestine or massive diarrhea or something. She even told me beforehand that she was going to try this deadly scheme. I didn't think it was going to work, since he'd probably taste the oil and spit the whole thing out, but I didn't say anything. When I asked her later how it went, she replied, deflated, "Oh, it didn't do nothing but give him the shits."

For all those years when my grandfather drank constantly, my grandma, though never an alcoholic, liked to have a beer as well. I'd take her to lunch when she was well into her sixties and she'd asked me if I was going to have a beer. I'd ask her if she wanted one and she'd always answer, "Well, I'll have half a beer." Of course she'd end up drinking three or four "half" beers, but she'd never indulge herself and ask for a whole one. It was hilarious.

It was a madhouse over at their trailer. As crazy as it was in my own home, with my mother's life constantly in turmoil, it was even crazier over at Grandma's. It was more of a comic crazy. Besides a one-legged alcoholic husband, my grandma also had to take care of *his* mother, old Grandma Heuer, who moved in after her own husband passed away. The state paid them $40 a week to keep her instead of putting her in a nursing home, and along with Social Security and disability, this allowed my grandma to stop working in her old age. Not that taking care of Grandma Heuer, sinking slowly into senility, wasn't a job. They built a huge room adjacent to the back door of the trailer to house her. It was the biggest room in the whole trailer, like sixteen by twenty. When I stayed with Grandma, I slept on a cot in that room.

Grandma Heuer didn't know where she was half the time. I'd go over to visit her and she'd look right at me and say, "There's some middle-aged woman who keeps coming in here and stealing my sweaters." And my own grandma would chime in, "Well, jeez, Grandma, that's me. I'm not stealing your sweaters, I'm washing them!" Toward the end I remember visiting the old lady and she'd point to my picture on TV and say, "You know, that little girl comes to visit me every once in a while." I'd try to let her know that the woman on the TV was me and that I was standing right there, but I'm not sure she ever made the connection.

The craziness around there escalated at dinnertime. My grandma had a Mexican Chihuahua named Daisy that was the meanest dog I've ever encountered. She was solid black and had huge ears—she looked like a miniature elephant. Daisy curled up on a pink fuzzy blanket in the closet in my grandma's room, and if you were a kid, you didn't go near that closet. That little nipper with the giant ears might bite your finger off.

So that was my grandma's daily charge—a one-legged alcoholic, a doddering eighty-plus-year-old, and a pint-sized version of Cujo. It took me a while, but I finally figured out why both the dog and Grandma Heuer seemed to be getting crazier as time went on. I started to observe a strange ritual that would happen almost daily at dinnertime. My grandma, having fixed dinner entirely by herself, would call everyone to the table, and once we were all seated, she'd point out to Grandma Heuer that, like always, her daily dose of pills was sitting in front of her in her spoon. My own grandma would turn to start passing out the food or something, and Grandma Heuer would, almost like clockwork, look around for her pills in the spoon, get confused, and then flip the spoon on the floor, spilling all the pills. Who do you think would gobble up those pills within seconds of them hitting the floor? Daisy the deranged Chihuahua.

Now a six-pound Fido full of strange medication, Daisy would then make a mad dash to her pink fuzzy retreat in the closet and stand guard, probably hallucinating giant phantom raccoons and squirrels from all the drugs she just swallowed. Open the closet door and she would snarl at you like a man-eating pit bull. I watched this little comic scenario take place almost every night and no one really knew about it except me and Daisy. Only later did I realize this could have been fatal to one or both of them. Grandma Heuer's mind just kept slipping away, something the medication might have helped, and everybody just thought Daisy was the world's meanest water rat of a dog. That might have been true, but she had a lot of help from that daily spoonful of mind-altering chemicals.

Pills aside, dinner was always a treat because my grandma would cook a big meal every night, even after working a twelve-hour shift at the Round Table. Fried chicken, rhubarb pie, or when things were tight, maybe squirrel or rabbit, but it was always a lot of food, made with love. Sometimes, when things were especially tight, Grandma would fix possum three times a week. We ate our share of catfish, too, and lots of frog legs. The truth is, I always hated frog legs, and wasn't exactly crazy about some of those other dishes. Maybe that's one reason why I'm such a big McDonald's fanatic to this day.

After dinner Grandpa would retire to his recliner without even clearing his own plate and start to drink his nightly round of Pabst Blue Ribbon beer. He had a system wherein he would finish a can, then hand it to me, and grumble, "Go put this in the box for Vern to smash."

My Uncle Vern was still living at home at the time and that was one of his jobs, along with burning the trash and gutting the rabbits and other wild game. Vern would take the used beer cans, smash them flat with a sledgehammer, then fill up an old refrigerator box full of smashed cans and haul them off to the recycling center to collect money on them. The box, Vern fondly remembers, held 285 cans, which is a good indication of how much my grandpa drank. Vern would return the money to Grandpa, who would of course spend it on more beer. It was its own little alcoholic ecosystem and the old man himself never had to leave his recliner.

This routine went on for years. Then one night I couldn't take his arrogant attitude anymore and told him so, loudly. I must have been about eleven or twelve years old and not really big enough to take on anyone, let alone a grandpa with a mean temper. In any case, about the time he ordered me that evening to get him his third or fourth beer from the refrigerator at the same time I was to deposit the empty out back, I just lost it. I stood right in front of his chair and cussed him out. I said, "I don't give a damn if you're one-legged or crippled or whatever, you can just get up and get your own damn beer. I'm sick of getting your beers, while all you do is sit and gripe and bitch and moan at everybody." Remember, I was eleven and female. He must have been as shocked as I was with what was coming out of my sassy mouth.

My grandma's own mouth was hanging open throughout this whole rant and I remember my Uncle Vern quickly backpedaling into his bedroom; he didn't want to get hit when my grandpa started whacking people in the head with his crutches, which is what he often did whenever he got mad. I was afraid of getting hit, too, but I was ready to stand my ground. The old coot had just pushed me over the edge.

My grandpa slowly got out of his recliner and cussed me right back in my face. He then walked straight down the hallway of the trailer to his bedroom and slammed the door. He went to bed around seven that night and you could hear him cursing and yelling all night about his smart-ass eleven-year-old granddaughter who had the gall to tell him to get his own damn beer. The rest of us tiptoed around the trailer that night, afraid to set him off even more.

The next morning he got up as usual, got dressed, drove down to the VFW Hall, and ordered an orange Sunkist soda. He was apparently through with drinking and never had another drop of alcohol until he started dying of colon cancer many years later. He quit drinking cold turkey the day after I told him he was a loser. As mean as he often was, I think I embarrassed the hell out of him and made him feel small enough that he felt he had to change his drunken ways to maintain even a shred of personal dignity.

My grandpa remained more or less sober for the next twenty years. He was always an ornery cuss but he ceased being downright mean. He was even fun to be around at times. He was stingy, though. He hoarded money like Scrooge McDuck and if he spent any, it was usually on a new gun or set of tools for himself. He had a little can where he would stash $2,000 or more and squirrel it away in a secret hiding place. He didn't trust anyone with his money—the banks, the government, and probably his own relatives. You'd look out the window and see him skulking around the yard, looking for a site to bury his treasure. If he caught you looking, he'd move it around to throw you off the scent—he'd lock it in his toolbox, or stick it under the washer and dryer, or under his bed.

My grandma, on the other hand, would work three times as hard, pinch every penny, and spend very little on herself. I remember one time when I took her to see the Eddie Murphy movie *Harlem Nights.* She had saved up $5 for the ticket by stashing it away, a dollar here and a dollar there, and she couldn't possibly tell the old man where she was going. First of all, he would want the money for his can in the backyard, and secondly, he'd go completely berserk if he found out she was going to a movie starring a *black* man. Next thing he knew, she was liable to bring one home! In his twisted brain, seeing an Eddie Murphy comedy was like a personal betrayal. That would have set him off more than the money.

My grandpa wouldn't even watch black-centered TV shows like *The Jeffersons* or *The Cosby Show.* Of course a lot of things on TV bothered him. We all remember what would happen when a tampon or feminine hygiene commercial would come on. He would start to clear his throat and then cough like he was about to die. The coughing would drown out the sound so he couldn't hear about Feminique or easyday tampons.

On another occasion I took my grandmother to the movies at the theater in Highland, the only one in town. We were standing in line and I said, "Grandma, do you want a Coke or some popcorn or something like that?" She immediately reached into her purse and pulled out this mangled, smashed-up paper cup that she had saved. She started to straighten it out and as she was doing that, she said, "Here. You can use this. Now you don't need to pay for another one of those. You just tell them this is a refill and they'll give it to you for free."

I was both taken aback and impressed. She had been saving that measly paper cup in her purse for months, waiting to use it again to save the price of a Coke. That's how poor she was, and resourceful. If you took that same purse and shook out the contents, you'd find Sweet'N Lows from every trip she ever made to a restaurant, and napkins, and little packets of ketchup, and anything else she could quietly tuck away. Whatever it took to get by, she did. She was going to make it through, come hell or high water.

And amidst all the chaos and poverty, she found her ways to enjoy life. Around the skirt of every trailer they lived in, she'd build a beautiful little garden. She loved to wander the woods and to fish in the pond near her trailer out on Rural Route 2. She loved all animals and had a particular fascination with owls. She'd fill her trailer with ceramic and stuffed owls. That's another one of her eccentricities that I picked up on and maintain to this day—a love of owls. When on the road, I decorate every dressing room with a collection of old ceramic owls I've gathered along the way. They're like a good luck charm and I can't imagine walking into a backstage room and not seeing them staring down at me.

My grandma had a gift for animals. For instance, she was the only person in the world I ever saw who could hand-feed a red fox. She located this fox living near her place, and over a period of maybe ten to twelve years she patiently worked on befriending that wild animal until it finally felt comfortable enough to just walk up and eat food from her hand. She always had two or three dogs running around, a bird or two in the kitchen, even a yardful of geese at one point. The geese were mean—they wouldn't let visitors get out of their car—but Grandma loved them. She felt a connection to the natural world and a peacefulness that came in interacting with it. I hope I can pass that same affection for creatures along to my own daughter someday.

And she was a night owl. She'd wait until everyone went to bed and the house was as quiet as a church, and then she'd sit down to enjoy some television. She'd watch something like *Court TV* or *The Jeffersons* until three in the morning. That was her quiet time and she cherished it. Whenever she let me join her for these late-night retreats, I cherished it, too. She'd often decide to cook a full meal in the middle of the night and serve up cheeseburgers or a freshly baked blueberry pie. Feasting on my grandma's home cooking and watching *All in the Family* reruns with her at two A.M. were some of the happiest moments of my entire childhood.

Which is probably why I do exactly the same thing to this day. The only time I watch TV is at the end of the night. I crawl in bed, treat myself to a bowl of Raisin Bran—the same cereal she often liked to munch on—and watch *Court TV* until I fall asleep. It's almost like a late-night meditation, a time to do nothing and let your brain process everything that had happened that day. It's also a ritual that helps me remember my grandma and how much I loved and respected her.

My grandma's great dream in life was to outlive her curmudgeon of a husband and have a few years of unabashed pleasure. Unfortunately, it didn't happen that way. My grandfather became very ill with colon cancer and it seemed like he was going to succumb long before my grandma. Despite the fact that he started drinking again, and made everyone around him feel a little worse, she still took care of him like always. Then one evening in 2000, she sat down on the couch to watch some TV and fell asleep, never to awaken again. Apparently her heart skipped a beat and she had a massive heart attack and died quietly. There was no struggle. She had her lotto tickets in her hand when she died. She fell asleep while waiting for the local news to give the winning lotto numbers. She died, in other words, while waiting for a miracle to happen.

And Grandpa Vernon died a month later. He probably knew on some level that he couldn't live long without her. And as he was dying, all the bitterness, anger, and disappointment of a lifetime seemed to disappear. During his last few hours of life, he made a point to call us all in, one by one, and tell us that he loved us. I don't remember him saying those words to anyone in all the time I knew him, but he said them then and revealed the tender feelings he has always felt for his family. It was a grand gesture of healing, for all of us.

Well after Grandpa Vernon died, I came across his own little treasure box, a cigarette box, where he proudly stored, among other things, his Ford work badge. I also found a set of pictures he held on to for fifty years that gave me some insight into why he was so bitter about life. They were small black and white photos of the victims of Hiroshima taken only a few hours after the bomb had dropped. They included pictures of Japanese women, completely nude because the blast had blown their clothes off them, holding dead infants with their heads half-blown away. He wasn't present there himself, but he had fought in the war, probably took down his share of Japanese, and never talked about it to anyone. Vern would constantly ask him, "Dad, how many Japs you kill over there?" and he would go, "I don't want to talk about that shit." He held on to those pictures, I think, to remind himself how awful that war had been and the scars it must have left with him.

On the night Grandma passed away, I remember getting a phone call from my mother at four o'clock in the morning in Nashville. She was beside herself with grief. "My mommy's dead," she kept saying, "My mommy's dead." It took me a few minutes to even figure out who I was talking to, since I'd never heard my mother call her mother "Mommy" before. I finally got the story straight, and then I got out of bed and went into the bathroom and threw up.

The very same night my grandma died, it turned out, I had conceived my daughter, Grace. To me, this was much more than a coincidence, as I'll explain later.

My grandmother was cremated, as was her wish. There were only six of us at her funeral, the only blood relatives she'd ever known—my mom, Aunt Vickie, Uncle Vern, my stepbrother, Josh, me, and Grandpa. She had few friends outside the family, because she had no time for a social life. She was either working or taking care of someone. Her social life was her family. In a lot of ways, we're still that way. That's why Vern, Vickie, Josh, and a slew of other family members are so involved in my current life. We all learned a critical life lesson from Grandma—Job Number One is to take care of each other.

I have the urns of both my grandparents' ashes on my mantel at home today. I see them as a constant reminder of what my grandma did to keep this crazy family together for all those years.

After she was cremated, I came across a wish list she had written and stashed away in her jewelry box, alongside family photos, the death certificate of her "real" father, and the flag and other mementos from her first true love. The list contained items she planned to buy or things she wanted to do after my grandpa no longer had the power to talk her out of them. This wish list is as close as I ever got to a window into my grandma's private life and private yearnings, and that's why I keep it near me as an invaluable touchstone. Grandma didn't wish for a million dollars, a trip to Europe, or a new Cadillac. She just wanted the simplest of things to make her life a little more comfortable. She just wanted many things that the rest of us, forever hungry for more and more of the useless things that America often dishes up, would take for granted.

The top of the list reads, in quotation marks, "The Smile of Hope." The first thing listed is "Cosmetic Surgery," by which she meant getting her teeth fixed, not a Joan Rivers face remolding. Then there was an entry, "Dog doctor, nails, bath, and exam." She then had a little dog named Coco—this was many dogs after Daisy, the demented, pill-popping Chihuahua—and one of her dreams was to have Coco checked out, bathed, and then have them put little ribbons in her hair. She didn't want to look like a beauty queen—she wanted her little Coco to look like one.

Because she saw so many infomercials on late-night television, she picked a couple of products from TV that she wanted on her list—a Bose Wave "radio with built-in c.d. player," and something every American should have, a "Ronco rotisserie oven." And she wanted two other gifts for herself: a manicure, for the first time in her life, and a maid service to come in and clean up the trailer, once. Not every week—just once. The whole list probably added up to two or three hundred dollars in expenses, tops, but to my grandma, that was a fortune. She'd never dare spend that kind of money on herself as long as her priority was taking care of her family. Only after the prospect of Grandpa expiring would she even think of something so rash and indulgent as getting her fingernails pared and painted by a professional.

I learned a lot from my beautiful, hardheaded grandmother, but probably the key lesson was that no matter your circumstances, your burdens, and your tragedies—life is what you make of it. In many ways, you couldn't have been dealt a worse hand than Frances Heuer—no parents, no past, the love of her life killed in a war, a husband that was often maddening to be around, and few skills to rise above a life-long level of poverty and need. But she did rise above it, way above it—she had dignity, grace, and perseverance and she found contentment where she could find it—taming a fox in the woods behind her house or laughing at George Jefferson at two o'clock in the morning.

I'm sure that Grandma dreamed of a different, better life and in many ways she was disappointed with her own lot—she could see that it wasn't glamorous or, in her darker moods, probably felt that, for all the agony and struggle, it didn't add up to much. I just wish she could have only lived a few more years and were here today. She would see the profound effect that she had on all the people she loved and nurtured, especially me. She would see how her example, as humble as it was, inspired me to achieve more than I ever thought humanly possible.

And if that wasn't enough, all she would have to do was to look into the eyes of her offspring, including her great-granddaughter and namesake, Grace Frances, and see that, even if she didn't come from an identifiable family, she created one that will live on, nurtured by her spirit, for generations to come.

3

HERE FOR THE PARTY

Well I'm an eight-ball shootin' double fisted drinking son
of a gun
I wear my jeans a little tight
Just to watch the little boys come undone
I'm here for the beer and the ball busting band
Gonna get a little crazy just because I can

"Here for the Party"

Despite the hardships I've described, my life as a kid was not an endless nightmare. We moved a lot, of course, and there was often a lot of stress and anxiety wherever we were living, but like I said, I always had friends and relatives nearby to keep me semi-sane and make me feel loved and protected.

And I had music.

I can't remember when music and singing wasn't a part of my life. It's funny, because no one else in my immediate family either sings or plays an instrument or has more than a passing interest in music. The only person who might have instilled a love of music was my biological father, but he wasn't around long enough to have much of an influence. It was something that I feel came to me as much from the inside as from the outside.

My mom claims I started singing around the house when I was about three. Apparently I was pretty good at carrying a tune, because by the time I was four or five, Mom would set up little impromptu concerts in the middle of Kmart on a Saturday afternoon. We would go there to shop and find a Blue Light Special where a crowd was already gathered. Mom would then plant me on a box or something and announce she had a treat in store for all the weary shoppers. I would then belt out a Patsy Cline tune, a cappella. The crowd would go nuts. We didn't pass the hat or beg for tips. Money had nothing to do with it. Mom just did it for the reaction it got. She was very proud of my talent and of course I liked doing it, too. I mean, who wouldn't want a Kmart full of people clapping and cheering and patting you on the head at five years old?

By the age of five I was also entering local talent shows, most of them sponsored by whatever school I was attending at the time. Mom claims I won my first talent show at five. I don't remember that one, but I do remember an early one where I came in fourth and the kid who won first prize did a great version of "New York, New York." Don't think I had to be dragged kicking and screaming into these competitions.

By the time I was seven I was actively looking for any and every opportunity to sing. No matter what school I was in, whether in Greenville, Illinois, or North Miami, Florida, one of the first things I did after reporting to my new homeroom was to sign up for the school choir, or chorus, or any other creative program that would allow me to sing. If there was a talent show, I was there. If they needed someone to sing "The Star-Spangled Banner" at an assembly, my hand went up high. I was the perpetual new kid at school who loved to sing.

And if I couldn't muster up an audience at Kmart or at school, I'd make one out of the family. At any family gathering of more than five or six people, I'd likely find a hairbrush to use as a microphone and run through my repertoire of four or five Hank Williams tunes like "Jambalaya" or "Your Cheatin' Heart." Or it would be the other way around. I'd want to go outside and play and someone would say, "Oh, come on, Gretchen, sing for us, sing for us," and even if I were tired of belting out tunes that day, I'd do it anyway. At seven, I learned a very important show business lesson. Never disappoint your fans. The show must *always* go on.

Vern had an eight-track deck in his room—remember those things?—and I was forever sneaking into his room when he wasn't home to root through his record collection. I knew it would piss him off more than anything else in the world; I guess I was getting back at him for all those Indian rubs and wild rides on the wagon behind his motorbike. Vern, in a way, introduced me to a much larger world of popular music at a very early age. He had quite a stack of records—Charlie Daniels, AC/DC, Lynyrd Skynyrd, and even the latest album by Loverboy. Right next to the rock was Waylon, Willie, the Outlaws, Hank Jr., Ray Stevens, George Jones, Tom T. Hall, and Roger Miller. You have to be exposed to music to learn to love it and Vernon provided me with almost daily exposure to all kinds of wonderful music.

I can remember clearly when singing became something more than just a parlor game for my in-laws or some hurried shoppers. Again, I was about seven. My grandma had bought a console stereo on credit from a local department store without telling my grandpa; he didn't like wasting money on such nonsense. It took her like five years to pay it off.

I was at her house one day and someone played a $33\frac{1}{3}$ LP recording by Patsy Cline of the song "Faded Love." I listened to it and that was the first time that any song really got to my emotional core. It made the hairs on my arm stand up. It was like an electrical charge or something. I was absolutely stunned by it.

I had already been singing for a while, but the moment that I actually knew what I wanted to do with my life was listening to that song that day. My dream was born right then and there.

Later that evening, I was inspired to sit down and try to write my very first country song. With my grandma's considerable help—she supplied words I had yet to learn—I cranked out a tune called "Winter Love." I can still remember the lyrics today:

> I hate these cold nights lyin' in bed,
> Thinkin' about the winter love that you and I had.
> I love you dearly,
> I'm so lost and weary without you.
> We had a love like the perfect romance,
> Under the stars I was lost in your trance.

Grandma gave me the word "trance" to rhyme with "romance." I didn't really know what a trance was at the time.

Anyway, that was my first effort at a tear-jerker and actually my last effort at writing anything until I started writing songs with John Rich many years later. But I kept up the singing and the general showing-off. By the time I was eleven, I had expanded my around-the-house stage act to include anything I could pick up and memorize from television or movies. Gather the clan for Thanksgiving or Christmas and the after-meal entertainment might include Gretchen reciting entire routines from the onstage performance film *Eddie Murphy Raw*. These kinds of pop culture exercises would offend my grandpa greatly—they usually involved racy language, not to mention black people—but Grandma loved it and I got a kick out of shaking things up a little. Hey, I still do.

Music was not only a way that I entertained people and received a lot of praise as a kid. It was also the one thing I could hold on to when things got crazy, which was often.

It was my getaway. I had to find a new getaway every time we moved. Sometimes in Florida, it was riding horses on a Cuban farm. Sometimes in Illinois, it was playing pool for hours on end. No matter what was going on in the family and no matter where we had moved to and for however long, music was always something I could escape to and let me feel good about myself. Unlike a lot of precious things in life, you can carry music around in your head and always feel soothed, inspired, and reassured by it.

I have some very poignant memories growing up in the country that involved music as an escape valve. If I was bored, bothered, or just lonely, I'd occasionally slip out the back of a trailer with a jam box, or portable cassette player, in tow, and head out to the open fields nearby. I'd find one of those giant concrete drainpipes that ran under an overpass or just along a drainage ditch. They were something like four or five feet from bottom to top. I'd crawl inside the pipe, assuming it wasn't full of muddy water, and I'd plant myself with my tennis shoes braced against one side and my back against the other. Then, away from all distractions, I would turn on my jam box and sing along to my favorite music of the moment. In those days, it was most likely a song by one of the great woman country singers of the time (and all time) like Loretta Lynn, Patsy Cline, Dolly Parton, or Tanya Tucker.

During this little concert for myself, the drainpipe would resonate like a big echo chamber and make my voice sound a lot louder, like it was being amplified across a giant auditorium. I was so happy in that little hideaway. I was in my own little world, just me and the coalminer's daughter or that coat of many colors, miles away from all the uncertainty and unhappiness that was often waiting for me back in the trailer.

As much as anywhere else, I grew up in bars. My mother was by profession a bartender, among other jobs, and by addiction an alcoholic. Pretty much everyone in my family drank, from Grandma's "half a beer" to all the kinfolk gathered around the beer cooler or the Jack Daniel's bottle during family gatherings. And at one time or another, many of my other relatives had worked in bars, including Grandma, Aunt Vickie, and Uncle Vern. Since I was a kid, one or another bar, especially those around Pocahontas, has been my home away from home.

If you haven't gathered this by now, bars are the center of the social world where I was raised. It's where all the local news and gossip gets passed along, where people play out their private domestic dramas in public, often with someone getting punched in the face or kicked in the head as a consequence, and it's where a steady supply of nightly and weekend entertainment can be found. When you got bored, which was often, you could head to the bar for a little lighthearted company, a boilermaker, and a game of darts. It was like a recreational center for adults.

These little Southern Illinois taverns, dozens if not hundreds of them, just sit along the side of the country roads out there with nothing else around them but wide expanses of farmland. They were every twenty miles or so. All you have to do is get in your car, start driving, and you're bound to find one where you least expect, on the loneliest, most desolate stretch of two-lane blacktop imaginable.

"Hey, where the hell do you think you're going?" some suspicious spouse would yell to another at about 7:30 or 8:00 in the evening. "You know where the hell I'm going," was the usual reply. "I'm goin' down to . . ." (Fill in bar name here: Hoosier Daddy's, or Flicks, or Lenjo's, or the O-Zone, or the Leisure Lounge, or Mooch's Pit Stop, or the Rail Shake Inn) over in Highland." This last place was called the Rail Shake Inn because it sat right next to the railroad track and every time a train came through, the whole place shook and rattled. It scared the hell out of first-timers.

The bar of my particular youth, as I've mentioned in about every interview I've ever done, was a nondescript little roadside oasis situated on County Line Road in the metropolis of Pierron, Illinois. It was called Big O's.

One of only two bars in Pierron, Big O's was a perfectly square concrete building, maybe forty by forty in size. On a good night, when a favorite local band was playing or just a lot of people decided they wanted to get good and drunk, the place held maybe forty-five to fifty people. Pierron is even smaller than Pocahontas and the main activity there is drinking. There's no stop sign, no stoplight, no gas station, and no grocery store. There are these two bars and a little cigarettes-and-pork-rinds convenience store with no gas. It's not like you'd go to Pierron, catch a movie, do a little window-shopping, then hit the bar. You'd just hit the bar.

County Line Road runs through the middle of Pierron and separates the two drinking establishments. One bar is in

Bond County and the other is in Madison County. This is significant because it means both of them are on the fringes of both counties, which means the police station in each county, located in the county seat, is a long ways away. The local cops or even the Illinois State Police rarely patrolled out that way. Pierron was close to being no-man's-land, law-enforcement-wise, and underage drinking was not an uncommon sight. If a teenager dropped in with his dad to have a beer, the kid usually got his own mug. If the people there knew you and/or your folks, your chances of getting carded at Big O's or any other such place were pretty slim. I mean, come on, you're with your dad!

Of course, if there was trouble—a brawl, a car wreck, or, God forbid, something involving guns—the police came running. But that was a rarity. Mostly the trouble was one-on-one fights, and mostly those got settled without having to call the cops.

Big O's was owned and operated by Mark "Big O" Obermark, a man who weighed in anywhere between four hundred and five hundred pounds, and a dear friend to this day. Nowadays Big O, in failing health, gets around in an electric wheelchair and lives behind another bar in the area. When he wants to hang out at the bar, he just wheels his way up a cement ramp, finds his spot in the room, and plugs the chair in to recharge the battery.

I was about thirteen or fourteen when we first met up with Big O. We got to know him down at the stock car races in Highland when Aunt Vickie's husband, Eric, was down there tearing up the track in his favorite Chevy. Big O was a big race fan and a delightful guy to hang out with. We'd see him at the track—he was kind of hard to miss—then join up later at a bar to drink beer and tell jokes. After he opened Big O's, my mom started working for him and we all just naturally gravitated there because Mark was so friendly and free-spirited. Soon he was like another member of the family.

Then, at fourteen, I started to work in the kitchen at Big O's, fixing burgers and fries. It wasn't long after that when I started bartending up front. Given the circumstances, you didn't have to be twenty-one to get a drink at a place like that, and you didn't even have to be twenty-one to serve that drink. It was just another way that I grew up fast.

Mark's dad, Rudy, was also a fixture around Big O's, but you'd never know he was his dad in a million years. He was a thin little guy, about five foot four, had a white beard and white hair, and always wore overalls and often a railroad hat. He was the spitting image of Papa Smurf. He also worked hard around the bar, doing anything that needed to be done, from serving up chicken strips and fries out of the tiny kitchen behind the bar to closing the place down. The menu at Big O's was pretty much anything you could drop into a deep fryer.

My mom worked for Big O at one time or another, as had my Aunt Vickie and my Uncle Vern. Even my grandma worked in his kitchen a time or two; she and Rudy became good friends. At one point we lived in a trailer park where you could walk to Big O's, so it was our neighborhood hangout. Kids in those parts didn't have many places to go and waste time. There were no shopping malls or down-the-street pizza joints where you could meet your friends and goof off. Bars like Big O's were great for that. You could go in one of them and shoot pool, throw darts, play an electronic poker machine, watch TV, play the jukebox, or eat a cheeseburger. Especially if your mom was working in a bar, you'd just wander over to the place and amuse yourself while you stayed out of everybody's way.

I also learned at a pretty young age that it is a great place to watch people tell stories, complain about their lives, get into arguments, and just let their hair down and be themselves. Especially if you are a songwriter, you just soak up everything like this and are pleasantly surprised when some detail you observed—like a Skoal ring on the back pocket of every man who walked in the bar—shows up in a song fifteen years later.

I learned to be a pretty good country pool player from all those trips to Big O's and later used that skill to make a little side money when on the road with local bands I joined up with. There were times, in fact, when I made *more* money hustling pool than singing in a band. Men everywhere hate to get beaten by a woman in anything, especially something like pool that they have played day in and day out for years. That always made taking their money extra sweet.

Live music was a staple in almost every bar in the greater Pierron/Pocahontas/Greenville/Highland area. Unless you wanted to drive into St. Louis and confront an alien urban culture, you got your music not from seeing Bob Seger or Ted Nugent in concert but from seeing the local Bob Seger or Ted Nugent wannabe who did a pretty damn good job playing and singing songs like "Night Moves." The local musicians invariably had day jobs during the week and hooked up with their band mates to earn a little extra cash on the weekends. Even before I formally joined my first band, I would worm my way into sitting in with bands playing these local joints. I was only eleven or twelve at the time, but I'd be there at five o'clock when they were setting up and I'd slide up to the lead guitarist and say, "Hey, can I get up and sing one with you later?" He'd most likely ask, "I guess so, what songs do you know?" I'd answer, "Well, I know 'Your Cheatin' Heart' in the key of G," and two hours later I'd be on stage, singing "Your Cheatin' Heart" in the key of G.

Not that Big O's had much room for bands. If you packed people in like sardines, it was still a relatively small crowd, all of whom smoked, so the air was usually a wall-to-wall cloud of smoke. O had an ingenious way to make room for a stage performance. The pool table that dominated the back of the place was on wheels. A piece of the back wall flipped up and you could push the table into an empty storage room right behind that wall. The band would then set up where the table once was and when they were through for the night, we'd move that table back in place and commence a game of eight-ball.

Big O's was a rowdy place. There are bullet holes in the back wall, but they didn't come from some cowboy trying to even the score with his cheating spouse. It was just our way of letting off steam at quitting time. Big O always carried an automatic .25 pistol in his pocket and after the evening crowd left, we'd take turns shooting empty bottles and cans at twenty paces. If there was some drunk still there who refused to leave, O would fire off a few rounds into the ceiling as a wake-up call. It always got them moving.

The seven or eight regulars who held down the bar during the daylight hours were seldom any trouble. They'd just sit there all day, nursing their "mug of Busch," with little piles of nickels, dimes, and quarters in front of them to pay for the next mug. You could tell how many beers they would consume that day by the change they had piled in front of them.

But at night and especially on the weekends, there was always something going on—a loudmouth drunk looking for trouble, an angry husband looking for his wife, or maybe the age-old rivalry between hard-asses from Greenville versus hard-asses from Highland. Even in an area as unpopulated as that one, there were cliques in the bar. The old guys hung together, as did the roughnecks, the women who dropped by, the Harley crowd, and the farmers. Not that any of us were much different from the rest. We all came from the same place and we all liked to listen to everything from Merle Haggard to AC/DC.

The men who called the place home were often just strange. One regular, named Herschel, drove a piece-of-crap old Cadillac with a big set of longhorns on the front grille and he talked in an eerie, robotic smoker's voice. He'd mostly just laugh . . . "Heh-heh-heh-heh-heh" . . . between ordering up another mug of Busch. Then there was Mark, a good friend of my Uncle Vern, who lived across the street from us. He'd walk in the front door of Big O's, already drunk, go straight up to a wooden post in the middle of the bar, and start beating his head on it. He'd do that, methodically, until his head would start bleeding. Sometimes this could take a good twenty or thirty minutes. Then, as suddenly as he started, he'd stop, wipe the blood off, grab a seat at the bar, and order a beer.

None of us knew why he did it but we knew not to interrupt his head-pounding ritual. If you went over and tapped him on the shoulder during this event, he might turn on you like a rabid dog. Sometimes Big O would have to kick him out for some reason and he'd start beating his head on the door. O claims Mark went home one night, got his pistol, dressed in camouflage, and sat in a tree waiting for O to leave so he could take him out. O probably talked him out of it.

O claims that Mark was a madman when drunk and a sweetheart when sober. With people like Mark, you generally just let them alone to work out their problems in their own weird way. That's the way you dealt with most people who frequented Big O's. Whatever their personal pain—no job, a broken heart, a warrant for their arrest, the DTs, or just a psychotic tic like beating their head to a bloody pulp— if they didn't bother you or some other patron, you didn't bother them.

Bars are not the healthiest environment to be around, especially for someone barely in their teens, but I never much questioned that life at the time. I do think that being in such a place where people often came to escape from unsatisfying lives and bitch about their miseries, I picked up on their restlessness. I have always been restless. I've always felt like things could be better, that there was more to do, to see, to experience and learn from.

Even today, if I write a song, it takes a lot of convincing before I think it's done and as good as it will get. My mom's compulsion to keep looking for a new life around every corner probably has something to do with this. She let someone who mistreated her drag her all over the country so that she might find a better life for herself and her kids. In this respect, I'm a lot like my mom. I also knew that there was something better up ahead for me, and I was itching to find it.

Some of my restlessness came out as just pure teenage rebellion. By the time I was fourteen, I'd had more than a beer or two, smoked more than a couple of packs of cigarettes, and was already a dedicated dipper. I used to dip in class in school. During one study hall in Greenville, full of two hundred kids scared to death of the teacher, the football coach, I had a dip in my mouth and was spitting into a Coke can when he spotted me. He located my can of Skoal and announced to the whole class that I was chewing tobacco and since I seemed to like it so much, maybe I should have the whole can. He then proceeded to make me eat the whole can. And I ate it. Luckily I only had a half a can left.

Here's where I showed the stubbornness that I had learned from years of dealing with my grandpa. I swallowed the whole thing and then sat there for another forty minutes as if gulping down a fistful of dipping tobacco was no big deal. I wasn't going to let that bully see me get sick. I wasn't going to let him think he really nailed me. Of course, as soon as class was over, I ran into the bathroom and puked my guts out, but I had made my point.

By the time I was about fifteen, the urge to get away from my mom and stepfather and try something totally new had become overwhelming. The restlessness finally took over. I had to get away from the craziness of their unstable life, for sure, but I also had to prove something to myself and anyone else who cared. I had to show the world that I could make it on my own.

4

REBEL CHILD

I understand, why you do the things you do
There was a time, when I was just like you
I know right now, you think you know it all
There's no way that you can break, no way you can fall

"Rebel Child"

One of the biggest decisions I made before coming to Nashville was the decision to drop out of school in the ninth grade and set out on my own. My mother had left home at fifteen to get married and have me, and I felt the same itch at virtually the same age. Dropping out of school is not something I would ever recommend to anyone—there are very, very few well-paying careers out there that don't demand a high school education, and in most cases, a college education as well. In my own case, though, I had but one goal in life—to become a professional singer—and my gut instinct was to start pursuing that goal as soon as possible. The margin for error, of course, was nonexistent. If I had failed as a singer-songwriter, my only future would have been low-paying, low-skill jobs like waitressing and bartending, and a lifetime of regrets about never finding an Option B. I had pretty much shut off all other options at the bright age of fifteen.

Dropping out of school was not all that traumatic for me. In my mind, I didn't need the education. I was going to be a singer. It didn't really matter what I would learn in pre-algebra. I would have no use for it in my adult life. It's not that I hated school or anything—I actually enjoyed subjects like history and literature. It's just that I couldn't see myself sitting around a schoolroom for four more years when I had something much more urgent to do.

Plus, I was never attached to any particular school. Because we moved around so much, I never felt any school was "my" school and never developed a longtime set of friends I loved to hang out with, year after year. My family was living in Miami for the fourth or fifth time when I decided to leave school. My mom had to tell the state of Florida that she approved of me quitting and in essence signed me out for good. On some level she understood my need to strike out on my own, but of course she had no assurance that I would actually survive and make something of myself.

My plan was simple. I decided to move back to Illinois, live with a way-too-old-for-me boyfriend I had at the time, find some work to keep me off welfare, and . . . well, that's as far as I had thought things out. Some distant relatives found us a furnished apartment, I headed back to find work, and my boyfriend was soon to follow.

So, at all of fifteen, I bailed out of school, packed my bags, gave my mom a kiss on the cheek, and headed back to Illinois for my new life. I had a restricted driver's license that required that I have someone eighteen or older riding with me, but I didn't have time for such luxuries. I hopped into my Datsun 280 ZX 2x2 and drove solo from Miami to Collinsville. I wasn't all that scared, just anxious to start over. I had learned to drive a stick-shift truck out on a gravel road in the country while living with my Aunt Vickie at age twelve. Maneuvering the Interstate in a 280 ZX was no great challenge.

I knew I could survive on my own. Long before I left home, I had worked for spending money at places like Burger King. I knew how to get a low-skilled job. When I arrived back in Illinois, I landed a job as a hostess at Denny's for the breakfast and lunch shift, and settled into a new domestic life. I got my boyfriend a job with a roofing company and rushed home every day after work to straighten up the apartment and fix him dinner. If I had decided to get married about then and have a baby or two, I would have fallen into the life destined for eighty percent of the young girls I grew up with—a life of hard work, financial uncertainty, manufactured housing, and a future that looked pretty much like today, and yesterday, and the day before. I'm certainly not condemning that life—some people take it and turn it into something full of joy—but it wouldn't have been a life I had dreamed about. It would have been a life that I had backed into without realizing it.

Fate dealt me a different hand, and the messenger at the time was my stepdad's cousin's ex-wife, a woman we called Aunt Brenda, though she wasn't really my aunt. She was around a lot when I was a kid and when I moved back at fifteen, she and her two sisters in Collinsville became a kind of a second family to me. My first family was still in Little Havana, living their version of "the good life."

One afternoon Aunt Brenda dropped by to visit while I, the happy homemaker, was busy vacuuming the apartment. I had all the windows and doors open—it gets hot in Southern Illinois—and I didn't hear her approach because of the noise of the vacuum. I was completely absorbed in the work and singing at full throttle while I worked, running through all those Patsy Cline and Tammy Wynette songs I could by now sing in my sleep. Aunt Brenda stood at the back door and listened to me sing. She must have stood there ten or fifteen minutes. She was completely taken by my voice.

When I finally turned off the vacuum, she called out my name and it scared the bejesus out of me. I spun around real quickly and she just stood there with this dumbfounded look on her face. She said, "My God, Gretchen Wilson, I didn't know you could sing like that. We're going to book you a gig. I'm going to have you singing uptown by next weekend."

And that was that. She in fact did have me singing uptown by the next weekend. She became my so-called manager and chief ego-booster in those early days. She talked to people I was too shy to talk to and hyped my talent to anyone who would listen. If she hadn't been there to nudge me in the right direction, I don't think I would have done it myself, at least not right away. We all need a little push every once in a while, and Aunt Brenda gave me that push, big time.

She went down to the Hickory Daiquiri Dock in Collinsville, cornered the owner, a woman named Donna Magac, and delivered her pitch. "I got this little niece," she said, "and she can sing her ass off and I can bring her in here to sing just as soon as it can be arranged." They negotiated the price—not a fortune, I guarantee—and Donna booked me right then and there. Now all I had to figure out was what I was going to do when I showed up for the first time at the tavern.

Brenda and I immediately took off for St. Louis and a music store called Shattinger Music Company. This was way before karaoke machines popped up in every drinking hole in America, and even before CDs. We were looking for something to back up my singing so I wouldn't have to stand there and sing a cappella like I did while vacuuming. We found these cassette tracks recorded by a company called You Sing the Hits or something like that. On Side A, you had a song like Patsy Cline's "Crazy" sung by an unknown demo singer, not Patsy Cline. On Side B you would have just an instrumental recording of "Crazy" so that you could sing along and think you *were* Patsy Cline.

I started with nine songs on two cassette tapes. All I had to do was punch playback on my little portable tape deck and I was ready for stardom. Brenda insisted that I perform that first night with a certain look—a blue evening gown, not unlike a prom dress, a curly-hair-style like early Dolly Parton, and plenty of eyeliner. Remember, this was a shotgun bar in a strip mall. The bar itself was right in the middle, the bath-rooms were in the back, and there was a pool table and a dart board, like most bars in that area. A packed house in that place was probably forty people, tops, most of them old enough to be my grandparents. It was not the Grand Ole Opry.

The idea was for me to sit on the bar in my evening gown and belt out these country standards to the Happy Hour crowd from about four to seven. I remember that first night like it was yesterday. I threw up from sheer terror. I knew I could sing better than most people and had had the dream to become a singer since I was around five, but dreaming something and actually doing it are two different things. Looking back, I was probably a little too young and inexperi-enced to be performing in public, even if that public was three dozen inebriated barflies in a strip mall tavern on a Thursday night.

But I managed to pull it off, with Aunt Brenda cheering me on the whole way. I guess those old folks got a kick out of this fifteen-year-old belting out songs like "Stand by Your Man" and "Crazy." I took the money I earned that night—$75, I think—and went back to St. Louis to buy more music. Soon I got smart enough to put together song sets on one cassette so I wouldn't have to keep stopping the show to take one cassette out, put another one in, and cue up a new song. I would start a set with a Patsy song, then a Judds song like "Girls Night Out," then maybe Tammy, Loretta, and back to Patsy for another song. I'd put together forty-five-minute sets like this and just roll the tape and sing. Then I'd take a break, load in a new forty-five-minute set, and do it again. Though I was singing other people's music on prerecorded tracks, I started to feel like a real pro, right down to the curly hair and high-heeled shoes.

I was now a certified, bona fide "Kountry Kutie," and started calling myself that as a sales gimmick. I began to play the Hickory Daiquiri Dock every other Thursday at Happy Hour. Soon Aunt Brenda booked me into another similar roadside tavern, and not long after that, this You Sing the Hits routine took on a life of its own. Soon I was singing three or four nights a week and often doing four forty-five-minute sets a night. Technically, I added an amplifier, a microphone, and a mike stand to my cassette recorder, and I graduated from sitting on bars to performing on little makeshift stages about the size of a picnic table. It was really all the room I needed, as long as I didn't have a band playing behind me. And even though I often listened to AC/DC and other rock music in my car, on stage I stuck with country. Everything that came out of my mouth at that time in my life just sounded country, no matter what it was.

Soon this became my life—Denny's in the morning, housewifery in the afternoon, and singing country classics to playback on stage at night. Aunt Brenda's involvement faded as I became more confident of what I was doing and learned how to handle the business as well as the singing end of things. I concentrated on this kind of performance for almost two years, up until I was almost seventeen. That's when I joined my first band, and as strange as it seems looking back, it wasn't a country band. It was an oldies band—a modified doo-wop band—with the improbable name of Sam A. Lama and the Ding-Dongs.

These were local guys, trying to make money playing music any way they could, just like me. Now I belonged to a real band, not a karaoke band, and I was really cooking. I begin to sleep all day and play all night. At seventeen, I was a certified rock star, at least in my own mind. The Ding-Dongs brought a Top 40 repertoire to the party, the perfect all-purpose bar band music for any Saturday night drink-and-dance fest, wedding reception, funeral, or whatever else came along. Soon we got the offer of a lifetime: A place in Springfield, Missouri, called the Townhouse Lounge was looking for a permanent house band to play five nights a week, fifty-two weeks a year. We didn't hesitate when they asked. We were headed for the big time!

By this point I had broken up with my boyfriend the roofer, so I moved to Springfield and rented a place on my own. I was making $500 a week, a fortune compared to a hostess job in those days, performing doo-wop five nights a week, and making a little money on the side playing pool in downtown Springfield. I was a real shark by this point, skillful at both the game and at hooking others into a friendly little wager. There was always some half-lit good ol' boy who couldn't imagine some smart-ass chick from Illinois beating him at pool. I loved the look on his face when I cleared the table.

I was also lonely as hell. I was a long ways from my friends and relatives back in Illinois and didn't know anyone in Springfield. Big O remembers how I used to call him at 2:30 in the morning, right at his usual closing time, and talk for hours. I can't imagine now what we talked about for so long, probably just who beat up whom at the stock car races that week. I was working and earning a little cash in those days, but I was far from grounded in a career. I was still anchored, at least by phone, to Pocahontas.

The Springfield engagement lasted an eternity from the perspective of a teenager who had moved every three or four months for her whole life. We played the Townhouse Lounge for a year and a half before I returned to Southern Illinois. Actually what precipitated my return was not boredom or restlessness but a massive car accident that should have killed me.

At one point we took a two-week vacation from playing nightly at the Townhouse. The keyboard player and I decided we didn't want to stop playing, so we went out and found a gig at the Lake of the Ozarks, a place about halfway between Springfield and St. Louis. Our act was playing Beatles-style pop music with just a keyboard and vocalist; he would play and sing harmony behind me. We did this for four nights a week for two weeks and then headed on back to Springfield to rejoin the rest of the Ding-Dongs.

I was driving my same Datsun 280 ZX down the Interstate in the middle of the day, and I was drinking. In my half-cocked state I reached down to grab something, lost control of the wheel, and veered into the center median. The car flipped over, then slid across the opposite lanes of oncoming traffic upside down. It didn't hit any other vehicle, but it flipped again. The second flip took me maybe twenty feet in the air. The car then landed on all four tires on a frontage road next to the highway. It was no doubt the most horrifying fifteen to twenty seconds of my life. By all counts, I should have been seriously injured, maimed, or killed. By the grace of God, none of that happened.

The ambulance rushed me to the ER anticipating a concussion or brain damage or worse. The EMTs on hand couldn't believe there wasn't at least some internal bleeding. As it turned out, my only injuries were two black eyes from hitting my nose on the steering wheel and assorted bumps and bruises. I had to pry my eyes open every morning for a week or so. But I had no long-term injuries and I didn't even get cited for a DUI. There was no sobriety test taken on the scene and I guess by the time I got to the hospital and went through a thorough exam, I was no longer intoxicated or at least it wasn't a big issue with the staff.

I was, in every way, incredibly lucky. I was especially lucky that I hadn't killed a small child in a school bus or a family of five in the middle of the day, and ruined dozens of lives, including my own.

The Datsun, the very same car that I drove from Miami back to Illinois at fifteen, was so mangled that I sold it to the wrecking company for the price of the towing bill. I probably could have parted it out and made more money. I had scoured a lot of junkyards looking for replacement parts for that car over the years. But at the time of the wreck, I just wanted it out of my life.

I was nineteen and stupid. I'd been living on my own since fifteen but I was still too immature not to know better than to drink and drive. Of course some forty-year-olds have yet to learn this lesson, but that didn't let me off the hook. I had just cheated death.

And that lesson stayed with me, at least in song. One thing I slipped into the title track of album number two, "All Jacked Up":

One thing I've learned when you get tore up
Don't drive your truck when you're all jacked up

My mom was back living in Illinois at the time of the accident and had finally gotten rid of her tormentor a year or so before. That made relating to her a whole lot easier. She came to Springfield and took me home, God love her. I moved back in to her place in Pierron to recuperate. In my mind, this was the worst twist of fate that could happen to me, because for a nineteen-year-old with ambitions to conquer the world, there was absolutely nothing to do in Pierron but go down to Big O's Tavern and stare at the wall.

That accident brought home something that I had known for a while and didn't have the courage or good sense or something to deal with—I had a drinking problem. I started drinking heavily when I was sixteen, about a year after I had decided to quit school and figure out my own path. As I said, showing an ID in the many bars I frequented was not a major concern. The drinking age in Illinois was twenty-one, but back then no kids there, like no kids anywhere, waited until their twenty-first birthday to knock back a Bud, or a dozen Buds, in the same way they didn't wait until sixteen to learn to drive a truck.

At sixteen I felt like an adult—I had my own place, at least part of the time, was working hard on a singing career, spent a lot of time in bars and had even worked in them by this point. I guess if I felt like an adult, I could drink like one, too.

There were long periods early on when I didn't drink—I was never the kind of drinker who drank nonstop until they passed out and someone hauled them home—but when I did drink, I tended to overdrink and when that happened, I tended to black out. Alcohol, I soon learned, was like an upper to me. It didn't quiet me down or get me tired or depressed. It got me going. Even during a blackout episode, where I couldn't remember a thing the next day, I was highly functional. I would often drink, throw up, then drink some more, and still be reasonably capable of carrying on a conversation or even working.

Only many years later did I realize that I was a functioning alcoholic from about the time I got my first driver's license. This was a theme in my life, and an ever-growing problem, for the next seven or eight years.

Meanwhile, I was back in Pierron, living with my mom. I wanted to keep singing, but I also needed some steady money and again went to Big O. Big O's turned out to be my lifeline during this confusing period of my life. Having dealt with a lot of come-and-go help, he was very understanding when you had to quit and take off for whatever reason. Since I had worked there before I moved to Springfield with the Ding-Dongs, he knew I could do the job, even at my underaged age. When I got

Frances Story with Daley (*child who didn't survive*)
(© Gretchen Wilson)

Grandma's treasure chest
(© Gretchen Wilson)

Vernon T. Heuer and Frances O. Story
(© Gretchen Wilson)

The fish . . . (© Dennis Willis)

Grandpa's clock (© Dennis Willis)

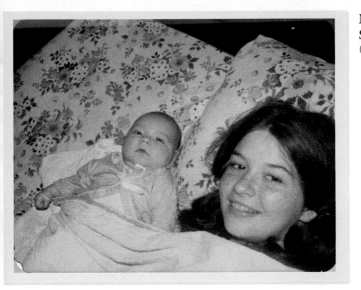

**Me and mommy—
Sweet Sixteen**
(© Gretchen Wilson)

Me and Mom—1975
(© Gretchen Wilson)

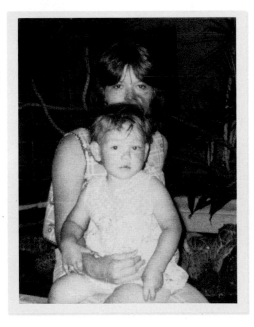

Mom, Me, and Josh—1977
(© Gretchen Wilson)

Me with Great Grandma and Grandpa Heuer (© Gretchen Wilson)

Me, Grandma and SunCleat (© Gretchen Wilson)

Me and Josh in South Miami, SW 127 Avenue and Calle Ocho
(© Gretchen Wilson)

**Me and Josh–
Lake Okeechobee**
(© Gretchen Wilson)

Fourth of July house party
(© Gretchen Wilson)

Diane Jackson and family
(© Diane Jackson)

Kindergarten in Greenville, IL–me (*third from the left*) **and Nancy Gaffner** (*second from the left*)
(© Gretchen Wilson)

Grantfork Bowl
(© Holly Henschen)

Big O–takin' care of business
(© Gretchen Wilson)

Me and Rudy Obermark
(*Big O's dad*)
(© Gretchen Wilson)

My Datsun 280 ZX
(© Gretchen Wilson)

Baywolfe: (*from left*) **Bobby Rolens, Craig Varble, me, and Larry Rolens**
(© Gretchen Wilson)

Fat Tuesday at Bourbon Street
(© Gretchen Wilson)

My first recording session with Bart Pursley. Still my engineer!
(© Gretchen Wilson)

Sign put up for me by the town of Pocahontas! (© Holly Henschen)

MUZIK MAFIA

Mafia–2004 (*top left: Cory Gierman, Big Kenny, Jon Nicholson, and James Otto; bottom: me and John Rich*) (© Marc Oswald)

Me and John at my first showcase (© Gretchen Wilson)

Singing with the Mafia
(© Gretchen Wilson)

The Pub of Love
(© Gretchen Wilson)

Two Foot Fred and Grace
(© Gretchen Wilson)

Me and John in Pokey (© Marc Oswald)

Mafia–2006 (*back, from left: Shannon Lawson, Cowboy Troy, Jon Nicholson, and Mista D; forefront, Big Kenny and John Rich*) (© Marc Oswald; photo by Joe Hardwick)

Me and Grace in Australia (© Marc Oswald)

Australia–February 2005 (© Marc Oswald)

London–July 2004
(© Marc Oswald)

Stockholm–July 2004
(© Marc Oswald)

Australia–February 2005
(© Marc Oswald)

back and sufficiently recovered from the auto wreck, I really needed the work and he gave it to me. Working behind the bar at Big O's gave me the chance to get back on my feet and start looking around for other bands to play with. Given my need to succeed, it didn't take long.

You don't get rich working in a bar. You usually get a small salary but your main income is found in the tip jar at the end of the evening. It's hard to keep steady help in a bar because it's a tough, often depressing life and attracts a workforce that is transitory, anxious to find a better deal around the corner. I was helpful to Big O because I could fill in just about anywhere. In the many off-and-on periods I was employed there, I tended bar, waited tables, fried burgers in the kitchen, did my karaoke routine in my early singing days, and sat in with the bands that Big O would book. I had my favorites, of course, like the Chapman Brothers, led by brothers Jerry and Jeff Chapman. They were the premier Southern-rock, Lynyrd Skynyrd–inspired band in the whole area. I couldn't wait for them to show up at Big O's.

The ratio of men to women at Big O's was about five to one, which only increased the odds that two drunks would start arguing about the St. Louis Cardinals and end up duking it out. My Uncle Vern had a lot of jobs around Big O's—bartending, cleaning up, moving the pool table back and forth—but on Saturday nights, he was the closest thing to security we had. He'd stand on a chair and watch the crowd and as soon as he spotted an angry word or a fist flying, he was right there to move it outside.

Working at O's, I got into the middle of a few fights involving women but never thought of myself as the female equivalent to Vern. Once I was forced to eject one of Vern's own girlfriends after she threw a big square glass ashtray at my head from about eight feet away. I had beaten her at pool and the drunker she became, the madder she got about losing that game. I proceeded to throw her out the front and locked the door.

Big O likes to tell the story about the time another bartender and I got into it one night after arguing about how best to dispense with an obnoxious drunk on the other side of the bar. A punch or two or three were thrown and I apparently broke the other girl's glasses. The next day, O got a bill from my opponent's father for $200 for a new pair of glasses. He naturally wanted me to pay up—he wasn't even there at the time—but I didn't have $20 to my name, let along $200. He went ahead and paid the man, but made me promise that the day I made it big in Nashville—Big O had more faith in me than almost anyone—I would pay him back the two hundred bucks.

Cut ahead a few years to the making of the first video to my first single, "Redneck Woman." I invited Big O to Nashville to be in the video and he remembers someone knocking on the door of his motel room and handing him $250 in cash. He'd completely forgotten about those glasses, but I hadn't. The whole incident was indicative of Big O's incredible generosity and I needed to repay it. The extra fifty was pocket money for roaming around Nashville.

I knew how to fight, that's for sure, but I didn't learn it at Big O's. Growing up where I did, fighting between women wasn't that unusual, especially when alcohol was involved, which was pretty much always. After once having my ear almost torn off when someone yanked an earring out of it, my setup line for a fight was often, "Don't make me take my earrings out." That was the signal that I was ready for a fight. It hurt like hell to have one of those earrings ripped out. Removing them was like ringing the bell for Round One.

A lot of the women who hung around a place like O's were very troubled. They were usually on their own after freeing themselves from an abusive relationship. Some found good jobs, as I said, but a lot of them were on welfare and had three or four kids to provide for. Like my mom, they might work a bar or waitress job a couple of nights of week to earn tip money, but they had few job skills, few job prospects, and a lot of problems to weigh them down. They saw themselves as stuck in the Greenville or Carlyle or Pocahontas version of hell and they drank to forget about it.

You rarely see these kinds of women on the evening news or on TV entertainment shows. They are, like a lot of people in Middle America, invisible to the public at large. Their voice is completely drowned out by celebrities and other types of TV loudmouths. And these uncelebrated women are exactly the women who I hope my music connects with and perhaps inspires to work their way out of the often tough circumstances of their lives.

If you were smart around there, you would befriend the toughest women you knew so they'd be on your side in case some real trouble broke out. While working at O's during this period, I played in an all-girl pool league called the

Busch Pool League. All the taverns and honky-tonks over a four- or five-county area would put together pool teams to compete with each other for a trophy or just bragging rights. There were six women to a team. We were known as Big O's Ladies.

Two of the women on our team, Big Kim and Jessie, could handle any situation, even those where men might be involved. I always felt perfectly comfortable entering a rowdy bar three counties away knowing that those two ladies had my back. Pool was a big deal in those parts and in a tight intra-tavern matchup, tempers could fly. Kim and Jessie were heavy-duty girls. I rarely had to take my earrings off around them.

As I said earlier, bartending is in my blood—it was the way my mom made the best money she ever made and the way I survived right up to the day I landed my first record deal. Having said that, it isn't a life I would recommend to anyone except someone who needed quick money for a short time. Given my background, it's hard for me to hate the bar life, but it's got a very dark side. It's a night culture and you become like a vampire—you only come out at night and only interact with other nighttime ghosts and goblins.

If I worked at it, I'd get to bed right before the sun came up. I'd wake up on most days around three or so in the afternoon and try to avoid the glare of direct sunlight until it was time to hit the Happy Hour at O's. And I was usually a bear to be around because I had more than a drink or two before hitting the sack. Daytime, in other words, was a bit hazy. There are more than a couple of boyfriends who've seen me in this condition and felt that morning-after bitching and moaning coming from my mouth.

Besides being places where I could drink at will, bars are full of worry and stress and strange people. You're working the third shift of life, filling customers full of alcohol and steering them away from trouble, while they are spending the rent money trying to forget about both the first and second shifts of life. In many ways, it's easy to see the bar business as the root of all evil, or at least a hell of a lot of the evil that plagues the lives of people living in rural and small-town America.

Actually, the real evil is alcohol. You can love the socializing of a good bar and all the friends you can find there and at the same time hate what alcohol can do to many of those people, how it can breed unhappiness and hopelessness and ruin lives. I've seen it since I was five.

Alcohol was built into the fabric of the country life I know. Not to be unfair; there are plenty of dry towns in Southern Illinois, and a lot of good people who lead Christian lives and have no problems with drugs or alcohol, but most of the people I knew intimately, including my own family, were drinkers. For the most part they survived, thank God. Many, many others didn't.

And running a bar can be as tough as seeing people drink their lives away. I watched Big O try to keep the doors open and it was always a struggle, especially given the fact that there was another bar within fifteen or twenty miles. As an owner, you have to watch every little thing, especially with a workforce that is constantly turning over. You have to watch the bartender who is pocketing a dollar or two of every drink before it reaches the cash register. You have to watch the cook taking fifteen meals a night home to feed his relatives while you're trying to figure out why you're losing so much on your food menu. And on top of that, you have the ATF and the cops breathing down your neck at the first sign of trouble, or the crazy drunk who pulls out a gun one night and ruins your business for a year. It never stops.

I've never owned a bar, and probably never will, but it is a life I know well and I have an attachment to it that will never go away. Bartending, after all, kept me alive until I could finally figure out what my true destiny was. And it taught me to stand on my own. In my life, places like Big O's were my high school, my boot camp, and my entry point into the real world, all wrapped up in one endless night of serving drinks, cleaning tables, breaking up fights, and learning, over and over again, that this is not how I wanted to spend the rest of my days on earth.

5

HITTING THE SMALL TIME

At fifteen I was tending Big O's Bar
I'd sing till two AM for a half full tip jar
Spent my youth singing truth, paying dues

"Pocahontas Proud"

When I was tending bar at Big O's and dragging my exhausted body home at three in the morning, I had no idea where all my dues-paying was leading me. After I got back from Springfield and recovered from the car accident, I was pretty sure I could sing just about anything, including doo-wop and Top 40, and I knew the lyrics by heart to dozens of both classic and popular songs. But I couldn't play an instrument and had no clue about what to do next. I had a lot of local encouragement, from everyone from Aunt Brenda to Big O to a lot of people who heard me sing after closing time.

Big O was maybe my biggest fan. He says today that he never had a moment's doubt that I'd make it big. He was so sure of my future success that he used to put up a big sign on my birthday that read: "Happy Birthday, Gretchen. She's Special." Special or not, I had no career-making moves plotted out. My one and only strategy was to find a local live band that could use a lead female singer and offer my services.

Big O booked a band every Friday, Saturday, and Tuesday night. Almost every band that showed up, I would end up singing a couple of songs with them and making as many local contacts as I could. Pretty soon, between stints at Big O's, I was singing on a per-gig basis in three or four bands at a time—country or rock, it didn't matter, as long as they played music I could relate to. One night I'd be booked with a band called Millennium at one bar in Edwardsville singing some R&B classic like "Knock on Wood," and the next night I'd be on stage with another band called Deliverance singing Meat Loaf's "I'd Do Anything for Love (But I Won't Do That)."

I was so fortunate to live in an area where throw-together bands were both plentiful and in need of my services. And all the genres of music I was asked to sing—Top 40, R&B, even disco and doo-wop—gave me a chance to try out a thousand different ways of singing and in time craft a singing style I could call my own.

During that year or so after I got back to Pierron, I felt like I was doing nothing but drinking and biding my time. I was singing whenever I got the chance and working on my craft, I guess, but I wasn't moving ahead in any real way and my dream was no closer to coming true than when I dropped out of high school. It was like the Credence Clearwater song, "Lodi," about getting stuck there again. Change "Lodi" to "Pierron" and I could have written that song.

Whenever you read about music stars in *People* or see them interviewed on *Entertainment Tonight*, they never talk about the weeks and years before they made it where nothing is happening. Music careers, even ones like mine that look to outsiders like they happened overnight, don't just move steadily upward. There are dead times where you are lost, confused, and just treading water to keep from going under and throwing in the towel. As restless as I've always been, I hated those times the worst.

I tried to keep moving to keep from going nuts. When I wasn't singing or filling in at Big O's, I took another bartending job in the funniest damn place in the world. It was called the Grantfork Bowl, located in, where else, Grantfork, another forgettable little town, current population, 254. The bowling alley and bar was about twenty feet by eighty feet, the twenty feet being exactly the width of four bowling lanes. Up front were the bar area, a couple of tables, and a series of automated poker machines. Beyond the every-night bowling leagues, the place handled a lot of cash because those poker machines occasionally paid off and the proprietor had to pay the winners in cash then and there. Sometimes old ladies would come in as soon as I opened the place for business. They'd sit for hours, smoking their Winston cigarettes and feeding those machines until they hit. If I wasn't careful, they could empty out my cash drawer even before the bowlers arrived. I worked hard at that place—my workday was a twelve-hour shift a couple of days every week—I'd arrive at three in the afternoon and close up at three in the morning.

So one Monday night at the Grantfork Bowl, things were really slow and I was bored out of my mind. I guess there were no league bowlers or poker winners that night. Around eight, Big O comes stumbling in with a bunch of guys I'd never met before. "Hey, O," I said, "what the hell's going on?"

"Well," he said, "You're not going to believe this, but I had to go to court today in Edwardsville over a speeding ticket, and I ran into these old boys who I haven't seen for a long time—and they're a band!"

The men who arrived with Big O were all brothers—the Rolens brothers, Larry, Jimmy, Danny, and Bobby. They all had that long-haired, black-blue-jeaned kind of Alice Cooper rock and roll look. That night I hit it off with Larry Rolens, especially, and we exchanged phone numbers and began to hang out together. I went to see their band—Baywolfe—play a time or two and liked them. They'd already built a pretty big following in those parts.

A couple of months went by, then one day, everything changed. Danny, the drummer, decided to quit the band. His wife was about to have a baby and she didn't want him leading an out-all-night-sleep-all-day musician's life any longer. Bobby, then the front man, decided to go back and take over the drums. Now the band needed a replacement front person, someone to sing lead. Since Larry and I were pretty tight by then, he asked me to join the band. Instantly the all-male rock and roll band had a chick singer.

Baywolfe became my permanent gig for the next three years or so. I celebrated my twenty-first birthday with Baywolfe on stage somewhere. Larry and I started living together early in my Baywolfe stint, which drew me even closer to the band. Baywolfe was actually two bands—the rock version, the busier of the two groups, was Baywolfe, but we also booked ourselves as a country band called Midnight Flyer. Baywolfe might play three or four times a week for every one time for Midnight Flyer. Same group, different audience.

Over time, Baywolfe became one of the most sought-after bands in the greater St. Louis and Southern Illinois area. We played almost exclusively in bars and music clubs and never in arenas or on the lucrative state fair circuit. We had about a dozen places we played pretty regularly and made our own circuit going from one to another and back again. It was fun. We'd travel all over the region, as far east as Effingham, Illinois, near the Indiana border, and as far south as Sainte Genevieve and Bonne Terre in southern Missouri. We sometimes played rock clubs holding up to two thousand rowdy people. I had come a long way, at least in my own mind, from singing to playback at Happy Hour at the Hickory Daiquiri Dock. I was a certified bi-state, small-time rock star.

Well, kind of. Our principal mode of transportation was a big, old, beat-up, used yellow Ryder truck. Sometimes it would take an hour to start the thing before we went anywhere, and when we got to the venue, we all unloaded the truck together. We were our own roadies, except for Bobby, who was usually working a day job and got to the gig only minutes before we began. It was my job, among others, to set up Bobby's drums every night. And string cable, wire amps, make patch cords, i.e., all the things that a crew would do. After the show, no matter how tired we were, we put all that equipment back on the truck and dragged ourselves back home. It was not a glamorous life.

But we loved to play. We would normally share a dressing room the size of a broom closet, put on our spandex outfits, apply some freakish makeup, spray our hair into Alice Cooper proportions, and hit the stage. This was the early 1990s and we were a badass rock and roll band, ready to blow you away.

The biggest place I think we ever played was called Pop's, a twenty-four-hour bar in a town just over the river from St. Louis called Sauget (pronounced "So-jay"). It was a short drive from home, maybe thirty-five minutes. The town is all industrial, a few factories interrupted by strip clubs and nightclubs. Because of a local Monsanto chemical plant, there was a smell in the air in Sauget that was damn close to cat urine. I remember wearing my best leather jacket on stage at Pop's one night and by the time I got home, it was ruined from that smell. I took it to the cleaners and they said, "Sorry, we can't remove cat urine from leather." I tried to explain that it wasn't cat urine, but it didn't really matter. Goodbye, jacket.

On a good night, Pop's held 3,500 people, a lot of them dropping by after all the other bars along the Mississippi

River landing had shut down. When we played at Pop's, we played seven sets a night. We started around 10:30 and played until 5:30 in the morning. Pop's was open all day and night, every day of the year. And people came late. Sometimes there would be maybe ten customers for the first set or two, which is like playing for the staff in a place that held 3,500. By the third set, the place was packed.

One night we were playing at a place called the Orris Theater in Sainte Genevieve, Missouri. It was an old movie theater where they removed the screen and erected a small stage for bands like us. Since we were rock and roll showmen, we had to have a little pyrotechnics, or fireworks. Our pyro man was a guy named Boone who pretty much taught himself how to put together small stage explosions. On that particular night, as most nights, some crowd-pleasing pyro was supposed to go off in the middle of the AC/DC song we played, "Thunderstruck." The blast was cued to come right on the syllable "struck." Very professional.

The blast came all right, but at about ten times the normal force. Apparently Boone had forgotten the pyro for the previous night hadn't gone off and then double-packed this night's pyro by mistake. It hit Bobby the drummer the hardest. The initial impact blew his hair straight out—he looked like a troll doll or maybe a white Don King—and he was completely knocked off his drum stand. The snare drum caught on fire and the rest of the drum kit flew off in six different directions.

After the initial shock waves, we just gathered up Bobby and what was left of his drum set, and continued with the show. We weren't about to let a small atomic blast keep us from finishing the set and getting paid for the night.

As Baywolfe rolled along, Larry Rolens and I became engaged. It was like the brothers that I played with every night were a legitimate family and I wanted to join the clan. This didn't always make things easier. One night as we were tearing down the stage after a show, Larry and I got into an argument. It got pretty heated and at one point Larry's brother Jimmy, who is about six feet two and weighed well over 250 pounds in those days, decided to intercede. He walked up to me and said, "I ain't gonna have you talking to my brother like that no more." Hot-tempered country girl that I was, I turned around and slapped him. He stuck his arm out and grabbed my head to keep my fists from hitting him, but I got a couple of good licks in anyway. Of course, if he had felt the urge, he could have broken me like a stick. Good thing he let it pass.

But fights like that were rare and the gigs were plentiful. Looking back, I don't know how I did all that singing, night after night. When we played at Pop's, I was singing four times as much as I do in a single concert now, plus I was straining my voice just to hear myself over the guitar amps and other noise on stage. In those days we didn't have ear monitors to modulate our performance. I could have easily damaged my voice pushing it like that, night after night, in places where the air was completely smoke-filled. Thank God I didn't.

Today, I usually play a ninety-minute show, without intermission, plus another forty-five minutes or so during the sound check for that show. Compare that to the six or seven hours a night I used to sing at Pop's. That was the singing equivalent of running a marathon nightly. But it was great training. Even today, I try to keep singing as constantly as I can so that my voice stays in shape. It's the same as with hitting a baseball or throwing a football. If I have ten or eleven days off the road, my voice is going to suffer. It takes a performance or two to get it humming again.

In a purely athletic sense, my voice just got stronger and more flexible. I have tape recordings of my singing that go all the way back to fourteen. Boy, has my voice changed. In the beginning, I sounded like Michael Jackson—high-pitched with a really heavy vibrato, or quiver, in my voice. Over time, my voice dropped and the vibrato started to disappear. And that came from continuous vocal exercising and learning how to do new things while singing cover songs of every possible style and technique. When you go from an Ann Wilson song to a Mariah Carey song to a Janis Joplin song in one set, you are covering a lot of musical ground. I sing what is known as country today, but my vocal education includes some lessons never taught by pure country singers, along with a whole lot of lessons taught only by pure country singers. Like a lot of performers starting out today, I learned to draw from whatever seemed right for my voice and the song.

My first assignment upon joining Baywolfe was to learn how to play something—guitar, piano, something—since the guy I was replacing—the front man—played everything—guitar, bass, piano, harmonica, even the fiddle. I had all of two weeks to try to learn how to play an entire set's worth of rock and roll songs. I didn't take too well to the piano, but I liked playing guitar and concentrated my energies on learning how to be a decent rhythm guitar player. I'm not a lead guitar player, then or now, but I've developed into a pretty solid rhythm player. Today I play guitar in about half of my show and of course use everything I learned about the guitar when I sit down to write a new song.

So the ex-front man—Bobby Rolens—sat down with me and started teaching me the relatively simple chord changes that make up most hard-core rock songs. That was the beginning of a beautiful friendship, both personal and musical. If you go to one of my shows today, you'll see that Bobby is still right next to me up on that stage. An incredibly versatile musician, he now plays electric guitar, acoustic guitar, and mandolin in my touring band. Bobby and I started out in exactly the same place with exactly the same dreams. Often when I look over at Bobby in the middle of a show today in front of a big amphitheater crowd, I flashback on our whole musical history together.

If you asked him about it today, Bobby might tell you that, at one point back then, he was pretty sure that life had passed him by. He married early, had three kids, and never could take the risk of moving to Nashville and trying to make the big move. Now he lives in Nashville, works with me, and has two new babies at home. He, too, has come a long way from those all-night musical marathons at Pop's.

The three-year period that I sang with Baywolfe was a major drinking period for me. It took a hell of a lot of energy to consume alcohol at that rate and still do three, four, and even seven sets in one night. As my singing career unfolded, I started to get drinking and performing down to a science. If I was doing, say, three sets in one performance, I wouldn't start drinking seriously until after the second set. By that point I knew I only had one more set to get through and even if I started to slip a little, I knew that the end was in sight. Plus, everyone in the audience was in the same state by that time, so it didn't really much matter. My usual MO was to finish the last set, then join some of my drinking buddies and keep imbibing for another three or four hours. I'd have a long sleep well into the next afternoon, but that fit right into the schedule. Sleep it off during the day, eat something, and start all over again. It was almost the same pattern of life that the nightly drunks at Big O's kept up, except I was also earning a living and having a great time doing it.

Larry Rolens was now my live-in companion and soon to be my husband. We didn't get married until after we moved to Nashville together, but we were as good as married for the three years or so that we both were part of Baywolfe. He was twenty-two years older than me and in many ways a lot wiser about functioning in the world. And given my drinking, my mood swings, and my ever-increasing frustration about not moving ahead with my musical dream beyond the confines of Southern Illinois, I was not the easiest person in the world to live with. To be perfectly honest, I was often downright abusive. For reasons I'm not quite sure of to this day, Larry stuck by me and took care of me during one of the darkest and most confusing periods of my life. When

I talk about men who let women down, I am not talking about him.

As much as I learned during those three years playing with Baywolfe, and the many good times we had along the way, I knew it wasn't going to lead me to where I wanted to go. I knew it was very unlikely that Baywolfe would emerge as the next Alabama or Lynyrd Skynyrd. I just knew that a record deal was never going to find me in Pocahontas, Illinois. I had known for quite a while that if I wanted to get to the next level, I had to get off my ass, save up some money, pack my suitcase, leave my friends, and relocate in Nashville. I was only twenty-three at the time, but I felt like time was wasting and I had to get going.

It was very difficult to break away and start a new life from scratch. In fact, for quite a while after I moved to Nashville, I'd drive back on the weekends and play gigs with Baywolfe. It was a five-hour trip one way and I was making it every week. I did that for almost a year before I said to myself, "Hey, you moved to Nashville to be in Nashville. There's no turning back now." I knew it was time to leave Southern Illinois behind and see if I had the talent, the determination, and the luck—or all three—to make it on my own.

But I never really lost track of any of the Rolens brothers I met that Monday night at the bowling alley. Bobby, as I said, plays about six feet away from me every night on the road. Larry, my ex-husband, now remarried and living in Nashville, currently plays steel guitar with the Bellamy

Brothers. Danny, the brother that quit the band, still lives in Southern Illinois, and Jimmy Rolens runs a bar outside Carlisle, Illinois, called Hoosier Daddy's—formerly the O-Zone—that he leased from Big O and behind which Big O still lives. I'm not actually related to any of these guys anymore, but they still are definitely part of my family.

I didn't just buy a bus ticket to Nashville, say goodbye to Mamma, and take off for the big city. I wasn't that big of a rube. I actually made a series of preliminary trips to scout the location, so to speak, and plunk some money down for a house to rent. Of course I had no idea what I was going to do once I moved in and unpacked my bags. I knew no one in Nashville, not a soul, either in or out of the music business. I certainly had no strategic contacts inside the industry, no letters of recommendation, no point of entry, no inside moves. It took another four or five long, frustrating years for me to even start doing something remotely connected to the real business of country music.

Still, the first time I drove into Nashville, I knew it was the right move. I felt something that I had never really felt about any other place before, at least not for very long. This time, thinking back to my mother's empty promise, I felt like things *were* going to be different from now on.

I felt like I was home.

6

NASHVILLE SKYLINE

When it rains, I pour a couple more rounds,
Till the hurtin' an' the heartache start to drown.
I turn out the light; I turn up Dwight an' I lock my door.
When it rains, when it rains, I pour.

"When It Rains"

It took me years to build up the courage to move to Nashville, but I knew I wasn't the only aspiring singer in America that was so brazen, foolhardy, or maybe just addle-brained enough to make such a move. There is probably someone reading this book who is about to clear out their savings, kiss their sweetheart goodbye, and leave their hometown in the middle of Oklahoma, Arkansas, or Alabama for fame and fortune in Music City. If you're aiming to be the next Steven Spielberg, you move to L.A. If you want to see your name in lights on Broadway, you move to New York.

If you want to have a career as a country artist, Nashville is the only place to start. Once you make it, if you should be so lucky, you can live in Hawaii or the Virgin Islands and no one cares. To start out, though, you got to be here, smack dab in the middle of the Nashville Dream Factory.

But before you buy that plane ticket, know this: There is no tried-and-true formula for getting a record deal in Nashville. There's no manual you can buy that will tell you the ten essential steps to get from winning your high school's version of *American Idol* to hearing your song played on country radio. Anyone who tells you differently is conning you. Everybody's story about how they got signed to a record deal or joined the legions of country stars at Fan Fair is different—very different. In almost every case, it rarely happens overnight and never as you planned.

The truth is, you've got to be a little crazy even to try. You first have to relocate to Nashville and figure it out for yourself. The rest is just insane persistence, and maybe a little luck. You've got to be determined, headstrong, and undeterred by naysayers, from your mother who wanted you to get married to your high school career counselor who wanted you to join the Army to the know-it-all record executive who tells you, as he says, "for your own good," that you don't have the right supermodel looks or the right sound or the right talent to make it in today's business. You have to know how to take no for an answer, repeatedly, and keep on knocking on doors ever after they've been slammed in your face. And even when they say no, over and over again, you have to leave them with a smile and a "thank you so much for taking some of your valuable time to hear me sing."

There's a famous hangout in Nashville that most hard-core country fans have heard about for years. It's called Tootsie's Orchid Lounge. It's on West Broadway downtown, a stone's throw away from Ryman Auditorium, the original home of the Grand Ole Opry, the mother church of country music. If the walls of Tootsie's could talk, they'd tell you a lot about the last fifty or sixty years of country music. Willie Nelson got his first songwriting job after singing at Tootsie's. Roger Miller, or so the story goes, wrote "Dang Me" while hanging out at Tootsie's. A scene from *Coal Miner's Daughter*, the classic film about the life of Loretta Lynn, was shot at Tootsie's. For aspiring country singers, Tootsie's is a mythical place, the doorway to the Land of Oz where all your dreams will come true. "Hey, do everything you can to get on stage at Tootsie's. Then one of the big record guys will see you and sign you right up!"

Unfortunately, it doesn't happen that way in 2006. It might have happened in some fashion to Willie Nelson five or six decades ago, but nowadays, it's about as sure a bet as winning the Tennessee Lottery. Those stories that will never die about sitting in the band at Tootsie's and getting discovered by Mr. Big are best left unheard by newcomers. The actual guys—the high-powered corporate executives—who have the power to sign you to a recording contract don't go to Tootsie's. They hardly leave their desks down at the office. If they are really considering you as an artist on their label, more than likely, you go to them, not the other way around. They might send an underling to check you out in some kind of showcase performance, and if that guy likes you, then they ask you down to their office.

I figured out pretty quickly after arriving in Nashville that it wasn't going to happen like a Hollywood movie, but it took me years to figure out my own particular "formula" for landing a deal. No matter what you've been told about the odds on making it in Nashville, you go there with high expectations. Things will be different for you, you think; all you have to do is believe in yourself and the rest will take care of itself. That may be true in the long run, but in the short run, you get a lot of rejection and it can be frustrating as hell. Get ready to be as stubborn as a mule.

My now new husband and I jumped right into the fray. We both went out on several auditions and came back empty-handed. We'd go to songwriters' nights at clubs or check out some local band and try to make a connection, any connection, that might lead to a little more exposure or maybe the chance to rub elbows with a mover or a shaker. Nothing seemed to work. We were getting nowhere fast. Occasionally, I'd try to sit in at Tootsie's and other well-known watering holes, but it was very odd and uncomfortable for me. In my mind, I was a lead singer in a hot regional band that could draw two or three thousand people in the St. Louis area, and now I was just another Nashville wannabe. On many nights, I was now trying to get an unsigned, run-of-the-mill bar band that was only working for tips to call me up on stage to sing a song or two. It was just too much for my fragile ego to take, I guess.

During that first year, I decided that someone around the house needed to earn some money for us to survive, so I went out and got the only kind of job I was highly qualified for. I became a bartender at a drinking and music establishment called the Bourbon Street Blues and Boogie Bar in an area of Nashville called Printers Alley. I was back to doing what I'd done since fifteen, pouring drinks, fending off amateur Romeos, and living for an evening of big tips.

After a while, I let the discouragement of too many slammed doors get to me and I stopped actively looking for my big break in show business. I said to myself, "The hell with it, I'm making $600 a week working in this bar and I ain't gonna worry about it no more." On the weekends I would get up and sing a couple of songs with the blues band that played regularly at Bourbon Street, songs like Aretha Franklin's "Respect." It was fun, a good break from long hours of filling beer glasses, but in my mind, it no longer meant I was on my way to stardom. I was just on my way to home and bed after a night of backbreaking work and one too many nightcaps.

I was terribly unhappy, needless to say, and considered myself a failure. During most of that transition period from Pocahontas to Nashville, I became as separated from music as I had in my whole life. I stopped trying to make up tunes while lying in bed at night or even keeping up with hot new performers. Except for the occasional song at Bourbon Street, there was very little music in my life. Little music and a lot of Jack Daniel's. If I hadn't hit rock bottom, I was close.

Then another life-changing event occurred, one probably as important as any before or after, with the obvious exception of the birth of my daughter, Grace. If I hadn't gone through this change, though, I might never have gotten to the point where I had either a career or a loving family.

One bleary-eyed day, I woke up after another hard night, probably around two or three in the afternoon. Not for the first time, I couldn't remember what I'd done the night before; I had blacked out. I knew that I had been very mean and verbally hurtful to my husband the previous evening, though I couldn't tell you exactly why if you put a gun to my head. I just knew that he wouldn't look at me or speak to me, a pretty good sign that I had stepped, or stumbled, over the line again.

It wasn't a big, traumatic event like a car wreck or falling down a flight of stairs that made me come to my senses. It was a look in the mirror. I went into the bathroom, washed my face and brushed my teeth, then just kind of stared at myself in the mirror for probably two or three minutes. I was more than a little disgusted. I was fed up with myself and the sorry way my life was going, and decided then and there to do something about it.

I was going to quit drinking.

I got out the Nashville phone book and started looking for a place where I could get some help. I landed on a recovery center called the Serenity House. It had a kind of AA-type walk-in (or outpatient) program and it was not that far from my house. So I started going to a meeting there at seven o'clock every morning while still bartending at Bourbon Street at night and not getting home until three or after. Needless to say, after years of working and singing in bars, I was not used to rising before the *Today* show went on the air. It took some getting used to.

I knew I was playing a dangerous game—in fact, I was committing the unforgivable sin of AA. I was trying to get sober and stay sober while I still worked behind a bar! All the other recovering alcoholics in the room told me that I was crazy and would never stop drinking under the circumstances. I needed the job, desperately, and I needed to quit drinking, desperately, so I had no choice. I had to do both things at the same time.

I chose the early-morning meetings for a particular reason. Many of the later meetings would either get too religious for my tastes or would often turn into giant whine fests. Listening to someone else talk about their miserable life didn't seem to give me much encouragement to turn mine around. If anything, it only brought home how messed up my own life had become.

The early-bird seven A.M. meetings were where the old guys, the lifelong recovering alcoholics, would congregate daily. It was a little like my grandpa and his group of old vets down at the VFW Hall in Greenville, except these were vets of the alcohol wars, not World War II. Some of these ex-drinkers had been sober for twenty-five or thirty years. Their whining days were long gone. They had turned their lives around and every day they didn't drink was a day filled with joy and relief, or so it seemed to me. They would tell these great stories about their current lives. They'd talk about very simple things, like the gardens they were planting or someone they encountered on the bus coming to the meeting. They'd talk about how blessed they felt and how their life was so much better than it was when they were drunk every day twenty years before.

Those were the kind of stories that would give me genuine hope and fortify my own determination not to let alcohol continue to rule my life. Those were the stories I would hold on to when I walked into Bourbon Street every night and poured $3,000 worth of liquor. These old pros showed me, through their own experience, what life would be like *after* I stopped drinking.

And, in time, it worked. From the moment that I made the decision in front of the mirror to stop drinking, I didn't drink again for two and a half years. I am not sober today; I drink, but I feel I have much more control over it. The period I stopped cold was the period where I began to find myself, and in turn, expand my range as a singer-songwriter, and lay the groundwork for the success that finally came to me.

Looking back, this was a massive turning point in my life. The lesson I learned then was a critical one. I was born an alcoholic, still have the capacity to be one, and it will always be that way. Especially now that I have a young child to care for, I am ever mindful of the damage alcohol can do to me, and as a result, her. I will do everything in my power not to let that happen.

One change led to another. First I changed a fundamental ritual in my life—getting drunk every night. Once that took, I made a big leap and changed the color of my hair. My hair is naturally brown, but from the time I was fifteen, ready to tackle the world, until one day in Nashville, years later, I was a bleached blonde. I was blond for all of those years of drinking. Now I was ready to go back to plain-old brown-headed Gretchen.

I also stopped wearing gold jewelry, my standard for years, and went out and bought all silver stuff. I changed all the furniture in the house and even went through and repainted all the door, window, and baseboard trim in every room. It was very detailed work. I had learned by that point that one way I could deal with stress was to throw myself into something that demanded my undivided attention. Painting a delicate window trim with a really fine paintbrush can do that. You're alone, completing the task on your own. It's almost a form of meditation, like any repetitive household chore. That's why I like to vacuum.

My Uncle Vern did the same thing when he was getting clean, only he did it outdoors. He cleared about six and a half acres of land by hand over the course of the two weeks or so when he was drying out. Bush-hogging, cutting trees, burning brush—it made a lot more sense than sitting around and staring at the wall, and he had six clean acres to show for it.

When I was twelve, I had seen my grandpa stop drinking overnight and cease to be the kind of mean-spirited tyrant he was during his drinking years. It was a wholesale change of personality. That was the same experience I was going through from the moment I walked through the front door of the Serenity House. I seemed to turn into a different person right before my own eyes.

Within a couple of months after this drastic change, I realized that my husband and I didn't have the same relationship that we had had during all those years I'd been under a cloud of alcohol. We seemed to grow apart, very quickly, and it became clear that our marriage, for whatever reason, had come to an end. Larry was, and is, an awesome person and God knows he put up with a lot of stupid and abusive behavior from me over the four years we were together. He showed me incredible support when I probably didn't deserve any. During a really bad period in my life, he gave me a safe place to land. For that I will always be incredibly grateful.

So I was now back on my own. I was working at Bourbon Street, going to morning meetings, reverting to the way I looked and felt before I became a serious drinker at sixteen. My dream was still light-years away and I thought about it less and less. I had a demo tape to hand out if anyone cared. They weren't exactly lining up for a copy.

I guess the reality of making it in Nashville was starting to set in at that point. I knew the odds were long. If I were asked to calculate those odds, I'd have to say that out of every hundred people who come to town like I did—no money, no contacts, just some talent and a dream that won't die— probably seventy of them finally get discouraged enough to go back home and try to find a different life. The three or four months they spent in Nashville trying to be a big star are just something they'll tell their grandkids. Twenty of the initial hundred probably stick around town and find some kind of job—just like I did—to make a living, to "maintain," while they keep looking for a way into the business. There are probably people in town who have been teaching, or working in an office, or tending bar for twenty or thirty years and still harbor the fantasy that the next country song they write in their spare time, or the next showcase they do for free, is going to be the one that does it for them. You've got to admire their tenacity, but their real-world chances of turning that corner are pretty slim. Nevertheless, it's usually from this group, the stubborn ones, that someone breaks through and makes it.

The last ten of the original hundred probably lose everything they have in chasing their dream. They often get hooked on drugs or alcohol, lose touch with the people they left behind in Alabama or Texas, and find the wrong loser crowd in Nashville to drag them further and further into the gutter. They may be able to sing or play a little, but they have no real money-making skills to get them by. In the worst cases, they pawn their guitar to pay for their addiction and end up homeless on the streets, telling some other wino about the time George Strait came up to him and told him he sang just like Hank Williams. There are a lot of these hopeless dreamers out there walking the streets of Nashville right now.

For a long time I was part of the "maintaining" group who were neither ready to give it up nor would allow themselves to wallow in depression and despair. I had a steady job, I had gotten a firm handle on my alcohol problem, and I had become a little more honest about the way I presented myself to the world. Despite the cynicism I often felt, on some deeper level I continued to believe in myself. I continued to believe that I had the talent and the passion to succeed. All I needed was to meet the right people, and after more time than I ever thought it would take, that finally happened.

THE MUZIK MAFIA

You know I'm here for the party
And I aint leavin' til they throw me out
Gonna have a little fun, gonna get me some
You know I'm here, I'm here for the party

"Here for the Party"

The minute I stopped looking for a way into the business, it seems, things started happening.

The bar I tended at the Bourbon Street Blues and Boogie Bar was upstairs; the bandstand where I occasionally sat in was downstairs. On a typical Saturday night in March of 1999, Stacy Michart, the lead singer in the house band downstairs, Blues U Can Use, called on me to come down and sing a couple of songs. It was about 1:30 in the morning and the bar was set to close at two. This was an end-of-the-evening routine that I was very familiar with at this point.

I'll let John Rich pick the story up from there:

"Big Kenny and I dropped into Bourbon Street for a drink because the band there was so good. We heard this woman being called to the stage and we thought, 'Oh, okay, the bartender's going to get up and sing.' Neither of us, truthfully, was paying a whole lot of attention.

"So this little brunette comes trotting down the stairs and hops on stage. Her hair is in a ponytail and she's wearing a little cutoff half-shirt and shorts. The first song she sang was 'Lady Marmalade,' and she just laid into it."

("Lady Marmalade" was a big disco hit for the group Labelle in 1975, around the time I was born, and another smash hit for Christina Aguilera and others in 2000. The chorus translates: "Do you want to sleep with me tonight?" I prefer the French version.)

John goes on: "It was like somebody had sucked the oxygen right out of the room. All of a sudden all you could focus on was her. You didn't care about your drink, your drinking buddy, the crowd, nothing—you were completely mesmerized, or at least Kenny and I were.

"When the song ended, I looked at Kenny and said, 'Was that as good as I think it was?' His considered reply: 'I don't know, but maybe we should pay more attention when she sings the next one.'

"She then sang her second song, an Aretha Franklin ballad entitled 'I Never Loved a Man (The Way I Love You).' Again, she just obliterated it. Kenny and I both realized, then and there, that she had this incredibly powerful voice that she had almost total control over. It was as clear as day—this woman had the goods.

"So when the set was over, she went back to the bar upstairs, and I kind of followed her. I was probably half-lit at this point. I was wearing a cowboy hat and a duster, or long coat, and probably looked to her like the typical wannabe cowboy lounge lizard/con artist with not a whole lot going for him. So I ambled up to the bar, got her attention, and said, 'So when are you gonna get yourself a record deal, darlin'?'

"She looked back at me with those kind of sharp, darty eyes of hers—a look that says, unmistakably, 'I could whip your ass'—and she said, 'Why? Do you think you can f**kin' get me one?'

"I said, 'Well, I can't get you one, but I might be able to help you get one.'

"Without skipping a beat, she reached into her purse, grabbed a homemade CD, and slid it across the bar to me. 'Listen to that,' she said. 'But I'm busy and can't talk right now. So either order a drink or get out of my face.' She then looked right past me at the guy standing behind me, and said, 'Hey, you want another beer?' In other words, she completely blew me off."

John is right. I did blow him off exactly for the reasons he said. He did look like a cowboy Romeo trying to hit on me, and in my job, I got that maybe fifty times a night. Plus, I had no idea who he was. At that point, John Rich was already a well-known and highly respected singer-songwriter in Nashville. He was a member of the group Lonestar and had just recently hooked up with Big Kenny—who he saw performing with the group LuvjOi—to form the soon-to-be breakthrough duo Big & Rich. John thought Kenny was a wacko when he first saw him and probably thought I was a surly bitch with a permanent chip on my shoulder. Of course John was someone I should have jumped at the chance of meeting and even working with, but what did I know? I was just a bartender with a good voice who hadn't gotten a nibble after two years in Nashville.

John listened to my demo and liked it enough to call me to figure out something to do together. I didn't call him back. I thought he was full of crap. He claims he kept calling every three days for close to a month. Finally, he talked to another waitress at the bar who knew who he was and she came to me and said, "Call John Rich back. He's legit. He wants to work with you. He's not trying to pick you up and he's not a stalker."

I finally called back, we got together, and there was the start of a long and fruitful friendship with both Big & Rich and a whole lot of other talented singers and songwriters.

John and Kenny were like a lot of promising but unsigned talent in Nashville at the time—they were disillusioned by the way the business was run and frustrated by the fact that safe, mainstream choices seemed to dominate every record deal. John had just been dropped by a label as a solo artist and Kenny was $140,000 in debt on his credit card. But unlike most singer-songwriters in the cold, hard world of Music City, they decided to do something about it.

Together with two other local troublemakers—Jon Nicholson and Cory Gierman—they formed a loose association called the Muzik Mafia. "Mafia" stood for "Musically Artistic Friends in Alliance." The idea was that a group of like-minded souls would get together on a regular basis, bounce ideas off each other, play original songs for each other, and get honest, sometimes brutal, feedback. If the record companies wouldn't pay attention to them, at least at the moment, they would pay attention to themselves. And the idea took off. What started out as just a circle of talented and ambitious friends—a kind of musical support group—soon became a legitimate Nashville scene. Early on there were maybe ten strange people who showed up at a Muzik Mafia gig. A year later the place we played was a fire hazard. The "Godfathers" of music staked out a unique territory in the country music biz.

Soon after I met John Rich and Big Kenny and started to hang out with them, they asked me to join the group. Other women occasionally sat in or wrote songs with the others, but I became the only official Mafia "Godmother." Just like when I joined Baywolfe five or six years before, now the Muzik Mafia had a chick singer.

I can distinctly remember when John Rich first started introducing me to his friends. He'd say things like, "You've got to listen to this girl. You just got to listen to her. She's twenty-seven, she's skinny, she's this, she's that . . ." and then he'd always end with "... and she ain't ugly." Not "beautiful" or "good-looking" or even "attractive"—just, "she ain't ugly." He would tell people that I was just about the only chick tough enough to be in the Mafia. The truth is, we were pretty hard-core with each other. In a business where people lie constantly, we thought the best service we could provide each other was to tell the truth, especially about our music. If someone didn't like a song that someone else had written, he or she just said so without mincing words. "That song sucks."

Cory Gierman, the only nonmusician in the group, did a lot of the planning and strategizing for the Mafia. He was actually a song plugger for Universal Publishing. A song plugger is a guy who pitches new songs to established artists in the hope that they will record them, and thus make the publisher, and maybe the songwriter, rich. It's a huge business in Nashville. Anyway, Cory had the brilliant idea of taking the Mafia into a public arena so that like-minded music lovers had a chance to hear some new and often outrageous music. On top of that, if the Mafia could create a good buzz about what they were up to, maybe even a few progressive decision-makers in the industry might take notice.

Soon the Muzik Mafia had a standing showtime and showplace—every Tuesday night at a little bar called the Pub of Love. I had to get someone to take over my Tuesday night shift at Bourbon Street, but I tried never to miss a single get-together. The Pub had two stories—a bar downstairs and a wide-open hardwood-floor room upstairs, more like an empty rehearsal hall than a barroom. Every Tuesday we'd transform the place into a funky living-room-type setting.

We'd bring in couches, lava lamps, carpets, rugs, and other such bric-a-brac, and do a little home-decorating. We'd vibe it out, so to speak, so it would fit our style and mood.

If you came backstage at one on my concerts today and came into the group dressing and lounging room we hang out in before a show, you'd see much of the same decor—old furniture, candles, and as a constant reminder of my grandma's presence in my life, old ceramic owls. Throw in a little Jack Daniel's and hard salami and it's just like home.

We'd make the Pub of Love equally homey, then we'd sit down and start playing. We'd just trade off each other's original songs, and everyone would chime in on some level as the song unfolded. Someone would add a second guitar, someone else would sing background. Not only was I the only chick at a lot of these sessions, early on I didn't have any original songs to contribute. Because of that, I felt kind of inferior, like I was more of a tag-a-long than a fully contributing member of the group.

The one thing I could add to the proceedings was my voice. I sang a lot of cover songs, but more importantly, by the second chorus of a brand-new tune, I could come in and sing harmony. Doing that, I could support almost anyone's new song even if I was only hearing it for the first time. Until I started writing or co-writing my own material and singing it in front of the group, background harmony was what I did a lot of the time.

Onlookers and other participants wandered into the Pub by word of mouth and soon that Tuesday night jam session felt more like a house party. I was second-generation Muzik Mafia—along with a guy named James Otto—but because of the free-spirited, open-ended nature of the enterprise, soon there was what seemed like another player or songwriter on stage every Tuesday. At some point, Cowboy Troy—a shoe salesman by day—joined up and became closely identified with the group.

The informal motto of the Muzik Mafia was: Everybody is welcome, but nobody takes the stage unless he or she is good enough to be up there. Everyone *was* welcomed and a lot of talented people doing all kinds of creative work showed up. You could come on stage and play whether you were a singer, a saxophone player, a harmonica player, a drummer, or a rapper, as long as you were accomplished and had something to say. It wasn't Amateur Night as much as it was Talented Misfits Night. As John Rich once put it, "It's about people who are unique and are not afraid to express their uniqueness." In retrospect, I fit right into this band of misfits.

And it wasn't just musicians. You might come to the show and see someone in one corner of the pub painting. Or a firebreather or a juggler or some other kind of circus performer. It was crazy, for sure, but it all seemed to fit. On most Tuesdays, it was a strange and ever-changing mix of artists and mavericks and freaks for any city, from L.A. to New York. For Nashville, it was a whole different reality.

Imagine something like this: In a room stuffed with secondhand furniture and lit by lava lamps and candles, there are twenty or thirty people standing or sitting around singing one of Big Kenny's crazy, out-there songs. We're singing together, arm in arm, in three-part harmony, loving each other at that moment. It was almost like a flashback to the

1960s, though none of us happened to be around in the 1960s. It had that communal vibe, though, the sense that you were surrounded by people who loved you, thought like you, and made you feel part of a real creative community.

Compare this to the way most people in Nashville have to conduct their lives as they struggle to find a foothold in the music industry. They might work with a co-writer or another musician friend or perhaps a manager, but they often feel isolated, frustrated, and forgotten. It can get awfully lonely in Nashville when you're trying to make it on your own. Lonely and discouraging. During some very unstable and confusing times in our lives, the Muzik Mafia kept us all going. Because we were all in the same boat at the time, we were naturally inclined to support each other and help each other through the rough spots. I think it's fair to say that if each of us had had to make it on our own, only a few would have survived.

There are a thousand reasons why people succeed or fail in Nashville, some of them legitimate and some of them as silly as the wrong hairstyle or waistline. Mutual support from your peers can often make the difference between giving up and carrying on. John Rich remembers more than one conversation where I became discouraged and he felt it was his duty to pump me back up and reiterate that he and a lot of others were behind me.

"Just look at me, Gretchen, look at me," he recalls saying. "You know what I am? I am a rabid pit bull dog. I am not letting this thing go until you at least get your shot."

I remember, between pep talks like that, lying in bed and thinking to myself, "You know what? I'm not going to do this anymore. I'm not going out there and take a beating anymore." Everyone who comes to Nashville has those thoughts early on. Not everyone, unfortunately, has a team of like-minded supporters like I had with the Mafia.

We knew we were all good and we kept hoping that someone was going to walk through the front door of the Pub of Love one fine day and take some serious notice. We didn't really care who got signed out of those sessions. We just hoped one of us got offered a deal and then, maybe magically, the rest of us would get our turn, too.

To make a long story short, the Muzik Mafia turned out to be a big success and things started to happen for a lot of us. First Big & Rich got a record deal, then I got mine, and others soon followed in our footsteps. Jon Nicholson's debut album, *A Little Sump'm Sump'm,* was released in 2005. The Mafia established their own record label with Warner Bros. Records called Raybaw Records. "Raybaw" stands for "red and yellow, black and white." The Raybaw release of Cowboy Troy's first record, *Loco Motive,* is nearing gold, quite a feat for a black rapping country artist. In fact, Troy is the first black country performer since Charley Pride to sell this many records. Cowboy Troy's second album, along with James Otto's first, will soon be released by Raybaw.

The Muzik Mafia still tries to get together on occasional Tuesdays to play, but we now have to pick various bars and give our fans little or no notice of the occasion. Otherwise, it would be a mob scene. When we officially perform together as the Muzik Mafia, often to raise funds for a worthy cause, we can fill an arena or stadium. The organization's mantra of "Love Everybody" extends to all kinds of charitable efforts, from Katrina relief to arranging Internet access for inner-city schools. What once was a slapdash gathering of diehard maverick artists has now become an enduring Nashville institution.

Early in my Mafia days, John and Kenny helped me discover a talent I wasn't sure I had—songwriting. At the time, I didn't really think of myself as a writer—only a singer—and told them as much. I was just being honest, I thought. I had never written anything that I thought was any good. John proceeded to turn my head around about this. "Just because you've yet to write a great song," he said, "doesn't mean you're not a songwriter." Anyone with a story, he went on, and with the talent I had—there's no way that I didn't have a great song or two inside me. I just had to figure out how to dig them out.

"Okay," I said. "I'll give it a try."

I was starting to get my hunger back. I was starting to feel like I did the night after I first heard Patsy Cline singing "Faded Love" on my grandma's console record player. Writing songs as an adult was uncharted territory for me but with John's encouragement, it now seemed worth the effort. It didn't take long, working with John Rich, Sharon Vaughn, Vicky McGehee, and a lot of other talented songwriters, before I realized I did have something to write about and maybe even the ability to get that experience down on paper. It was a while before I got around to writing or co-writing the songs that helped launch my career—"Redneck Woman," "Pocahontas Proud," and "Not Bad for a Bartender," for instance—but those songs began to germinate in those early days of the Muzik Mafia.

Though it was written a little later in the story, here's how one of those songs, "Redneck Woman," came about. We were sitting around John's apartment in Nashville one afternoon. We had gotten together for the explicit purpose of writing a new song, though we had no idea what that song might be. John was tuning his guitar and I was watching CMT (Country Music Television) on his TV. I watched three videos, back to back, and they all featured drop-dead beautiful women singing beautiful songs. They were combination singer-supermodels and they were, and still are, some of the reigning stars of country music—Shania Twain, Faith Hill, and Martina McBride, just to name three.

John remembers exactly what I was wearing at the time—a wife-beater tank top, a pair of sweatpants, and flip-flops. I had no makeup on and I had a cigarette in one hand and a bottle of beer in another. After watching these videos, I turned to John and said, "You know what, man? There's just no way that I can do that. No way in hell."

"Do what?" he asked.

I pointed to the TV screen and said, "That. I can't do that. That's just not what I am."

He asked, "Then what are you?"

I replied, "I guess I'm just a redneck woman!"

Bingo!

"You're right," John said. "You are not the Barbie Doll type."

Right there was the idea for the song, and an hour and a half later, the song "Redneck Woman" was done. It was a song exactly true to who I am and the people I come from. And it has nothing to do with the racist, stupid, hateful, backward "redneck" stereotype that will hopefully, in time, disappear from the language. "Redneck" in "Redneck Woman" is a lifestyle, an attitude toward the world. It's about people who work hard, often in blue-collar jobs, and play hard. And they don't take no crap from anyone about who they are and where they come from.

"Redneck Woman" and other songs I began to write were part of a discovery process, I think. I wasn't discovering how to write a hit song in the conventional sense or how to come up with something that the record executives might see as a commercial winner. I was discovering something much more important—what really makes a singer-songwriter connect to his or her fans and build a career on a solid foundation and not just on hype, musical fads, or the right image for the moment. That's at the heart of country music—connecting with your audience on some level of real-life experience. The more of yourself you put in the music—warts and all—the greater the chance that the audience will take that music into their own hearts.

It's a simple-sounding lesson—be true to yourself—but it's a lesson that a lot of very talented people never quite learn; trying to please others to get ahead usually gets you nowhere. There are a lot of BS'ers in Nashville and if you walk in the door with your own line of BS, they can see it before you plop down on the couch.

John Rich has said that I probably spent too much time after coming to Nashville trying to hide or skip over my rough spots. I guess that's what the blond hair and gold jewelry were all about. Sobering up helped me shed some of that protective stuff, and when I began to realize that the rough spots were part of my life, and probably a part of millions of people's lives, that's when I began to write songs that were more honest and open. When you stop to think about it, a lot of my life was nothing but rough spots—learning to deal with all of that adversity and still keep going was the main story I had to tell. Now, all I needed was someone to give me the chance to tell it.

In the same way I had to learn to let a little more of myself out in my music, I had to learn a few things about letting my guard down and being more trusting of others. In some ways, I guess, my "don't-mess-with-me" personality was getting in the way, or could get in the way, of people embracing my music. Big Kenny's first impression of me was that I was a bit of a smartass, which I was, and not all that personable. As I said earlier, I had developed a pretty hard edge to protect myself from all the nasty, untrustworthy, and conniving people I had to deal with as a child. Big Kenny remembers having more than one long conversation with me during those tell-it-like-it-is Mafia get-togethers on my need to mellow out a little and not see everyone around me as a potential rival or threat. If that group of merry music-makers taught me anything, it was that there were people out there who cared about me and supported me and were happy to help me stand on my own feet and survive in Nashville.

As I say in the song "Redneck Woman," I'm not the sweet, perky Barbie Doll type, and never will be. I grew up with a pretty tough crowd and will probably always be a little bit wary of strangers. But, with the help of friends like Big Kenny, I'm a hell of a lot more open and trusting than I was when I pulled into town eight or nine years ago.

Looking back, Kenny now thinks it was a blessing that I wasn't the Barbie Doll type and couldn't pull off the glossy beauty-queen act with the soft, sweet voice if my life depended on it. I would have fallen on my face. I would have failed miserably at being something that I wasn't cut out to be and probably be back at Hoosier Daddy's right now, pouring beer. I could only be one thing—who I was—a redneck woman who still kept "my Christmas lights on, on my front porch all year long."

We were damn lucky that the Muzik Mafia gave a lot of us a platform to succeed, but again, it didn't happen overnight. I played Tuesday nights with that group of gypsies for another two years before I finally met the right executive who saw what I had to offer and was ready to roll the dice.

It's a truism but it's the absolute truth—nothing happens fast in Nashville. You have to wait a lifetime for one twenty-minute shot at stardom.

So I was bartending, learning my craft with the Muzik Mafia, and trying to stay positive and hopeful about the future. Then something else happened to make things even more complicated.

I up and got pregnant.

CHAPTER

BABY GRACE

At twenty-seven I had baby Grace
I was born again when I saw her sweet face
And I knew she was the greatest thing I'd ever do

"Pocahontas Proud"

I guess you'd have to say that the period where I had my sweet daughter, Grace, while still trying to both earn a living and get ahead in the music business was simultaneously the highest and the lowest point of my life. Personally, it was one of the happiest times I've ever experienced, before or after. I loved the whole experience of having a child growing inside me and then being with that child day and night for the first six to eight months of her existence on earth. I had Grace at twenty-seven and believe it or not, I felt I was pretty old to have a baby. Where I was from, I was a late starter. My mother had me at sixteen. A lot of women in Southern

Illinois started having kids long before they were twenty. It is just part of the rhythm of life there.

As I mentioned earlier, Grace was conceived on the very night that my dear grandma passed away, in fact, within an hour of her death, as I later reconstructed. I took that as an important omen in all of our lives. A couple of weeks after her passing and the small family funeral in Illinois, I started feeling really sick, put two and two together, and decided to go get a pregnancy test. I went to a walk-in clinic and had a professional do the test, and got the good news. I'll never forget the old man who walked into the room and said, "Picked out any names yet?" I about passed out.

I wasn't planning to have a baby, that's for sure, and frankly, I was a little scared. It was something that I had wanted for a long time but it never quite worked out. At that point it was the furthest thing from my mind. I had gotten the divorce from Larry only a few months before and was now seeing Mike, Grace's father, who was then one of the owners of the Bourbon Street Bar. We didn't really know each other that well at the time and neither of us were ready to contemplate raising a child together. Mike worked until four every morning at the bar and I was still stuck in the in-between place in my career where I had to keep working like a dog if I was ever going to make it to the next level. It was a very difficult time.

Initially, I felt downright miserable. I saw myself as fat and ugly and pregnant, in other words, every negative emotion a woman goes through as her body and her life are being taken over by a pregnancy. At the same time, given my fragile emotional condition, I started feeling that my dream that led me to Nashville was slowly slipping away. Muzik Mafia aside, I thought, I hadn't really gotten that far in the four years I had been in town, and here I was, pregnant! It's even hard to sing in the shower when you're pregnant, let alone on stage or in a studio. It affects your breathing patterns. You tend to run out of breath in the middle of a long musical phrase.

I felt like I was falling into a whole new life that I really hadn't chosen. The responsibilities of motherhood can easily take over a young woman's life. I saw this happen to girls all the time in Illinois; they'd get pregnant in high school by the boy they liked at the time, and their life proceeded to take a radically different path than the one they imagined. College was out, traveling was out, taking a few risks on their own was out. Marriage and babies and worrying about the next mortgage payment were in.

I didn't know what to do. I wasn't ready to have a child but didn't want to give her up. Nor did I want to give up on a career. I remember one extremely important conversation I had with John Rich about all this. We were sitting in his Dodge pickup truck, somewhere downtown, right off Broadway, after a showcase one night. I hadn't been pregnant very long and no one really knew but Mike and me. I remember this little heart-to-heart talk like it was yesterday.

"I'm pregnant," I said to John, "and I don't know what I'm going to do. I feel awful about this. You and Sharon and others have worked so hard for me. You've set me up on showcases, you've gone into the studio with me to cut demos, you've drawn me into the Mafia, you've talked me up all over town, and now, here I am. I'm pregnant. I don't want to let you guys down, but I don't know how I can keep on. I think this is going to be the end of it. I'm afraid I'm going to be finished. I'm done."

This was the moment of truth, I guess, where I had to decide what I was really going to do.

John is the son of a preacher. His father is a nondenominational Christian evangelist in Ashland City, Tennessee; he's a speaker, a healer, and a visionary. It felt, sitting in that truck, like John kind of turned into his father. He had a very definite idea of the right way for me to proceed. First of all, he said, I was ignorant if I was to even consider the thought of an abortion. I had, of course, but only for a split second. He told me that with all the things I had lived through in my life, all the pain and worry and misery, I was certainly tough enough to handle being a mother and having a career at the same time. If anyone could, he said, I could. If anyone *should*, he said, I was the one who should.

He was absolutely right. He convinced me that night that the right course was the hardest course—do both things at once—and that I could pull it off. That conversation was a definite turning point in my life and a bonding moment for John and me. Whenever I get mad at him these days, whenever I'm ready to throw something at him, all I have to do to calm down is remember that little session in his pickup that night. It forever reminds me of how close we are.

The first thing, of course, was to have a healthy, happy baby and give her all the love and attention I could muster. Mike and I made the decision that he would keep working to provide an income and I would quit my bartending job and focus on my pregnancy. It was a wonderful thing for him to do, and the right thing, too. Hanging out in a smoke-filled bar night after night is hardly the healthiest way to go through a pregnancy, let alone putting up with all the drunks and lounge lizards giving you a hard time. I went home and tried, without much success, to keep up singing and songwriting during those nine months. Mike brought home the paycheck.

It was a hell of a delivery. Baby Grace weighed in at eight pounds, six ounces and she had a fourteen-and-a-half-inch head. She had her father's head. I was in labor for sixteen hours and when it was over, my doctor told me right out, "You're not made for having babies." After sixteen hours of tough, tough labor, I understood.

Again, I had Grace when I was twenty-seven. Soon 27 became kind of a magical number for me. It seems to pop up everywhere. Stop and think about it. When I left Pocahontas, the population was 727. In the song "Pocahontas Proud," I sing, "At twenty-seven I had baby Grace." And what was my first week of record sales? 227,000 units.

By that point, I started spotting 27s everywhere in my life. The address to Hoosier Daddy's is 12727 Rural Route 127. When I landed in Australia during a worldwide media tour on the heels of my first album, it was the very first time I had ever set foot on foreign soil, not counting Canada. When the plane hit the ground, the first thing I saw out the window was a big meat truck with a giant 27 on the side.

And on and on it goes. I'm now surrounded by 27s. One night in Los Angeles, we got a little crazy and ran across the street from the Viper Room Lounge to a tattoo parlor so I could get 27 tattooed on my ankle. If you come to one of my concerts and use your binoculars to look at me closely, you'll see that around my neck I'm wearing a silver dog tag I engraved with 27. The people closest to me, on stage and in my personal life, are probably wearing one, too.

I don't really know what it all means—I am not a numerology freak or anything—but I guess the number has become a sign for me. If I go too long without seeing or hearing a 27, I might want to rethink the path I'm on. Maybe I'll have to do that around the time of my twenty-*eighth* album.

Remember that number, 27. It comes up later in the story.

Grace is of course the most important 27 of all. For the first six months of her life, I stayed home with her. I didn't want it any other way. I was with her every day, every night, every meal, every burp, every diaper, every everything. It would have been devastating to me if I had had to go back to work right away and drop Grace off at a day-care center, like millions of working mothers have to do every day. If I was going to have a kid and have a career, I was going to do it right, and doing it right meant giving Grace my total attention during the early stages of life.

I got the name Grace out of a name book for babies. I looked up every name known to man and none of them felt right until I got to Grace. She clearly had "graced" me in her life and love. Given her connection to my grandmother, her second name is Frances. Frances happens to be my middle name, too. We have a lot of Franceses around the family now.

At a certain point, I felt it was time to leave my full-time involvement with Grace and get back to work. This was a really hard thing to do, as every new mother knows. In fact, it was one of the hardest things I ever had to do, to leave my child and go out for myself and my own career ambitions. It felt self-indulgent and still does sometimes. In those first couple of years, it was physically painful to be separated from her for any length of time. I tried to figure out every way in the world that I could keep her with me, wherever I was. Then, as now, she was the center of my life.

Mike and I never married, but we were together as long as I had been with anyone in my life. As I said, he supported me both before and after the birth of Grace. Then, as Grace grew and my attitude about working began to change, we made a conscious decision to switch roles. As long as I provided support for the family, Mike would quit his job and devote his time to raising Grace. As it turned out, this arrangement went on for another four or five years. Mike was, and is, a great dad. The fact that I could be sure that Grace was in good hands with him really helped ease my mind during the period and concentrate on getting a foothold in the music business.

One way in I found, was the demo business. Demo recordings are huge in Nashville, an ongoing year-round cottage industry. There are literally thousands of both aspiring and veteran songwriters working on new songs every single day in that town. Some are holed up in a cheap apartment somewhere, working away, like the way John and

I got together to write "Redneck Woman" and other tunes. A lot of professional songwriters are in little rooms and cubicles in the big publishing offices on Nashville's famous Music Row, trying like hell to come up with the next hit for Reba McEntire or Brooks & Dunn. It's a tough trade being a song-writer in Nashville. It's kind of like being a Hollywood star, I guess. For every real star you see on *Entertainment Tonight,* there are thousands of actors struggling to pay the rent.

Even if you are an established pro, the work is hard and unpredictable. Published songwriters on Music Row turn all the songs they have written in a given period to the publish-ing company they are attached to. The publishing company listens to them and says, "All right, out of the twenty songs you wrote this month, we think five of them are awesome. So we'll reject the other fifteen and concentrate on the five we think might appeal to and get cut by a popular performer. Now we're going to give you, say, five or six grand to get a band together, go into a studio, and cut a demo of these five songs. And get them back to us by next Tuesday."

And that's where I came in. I was the female vocalist on the demos of one or all of those songs. Let's say they wrote a song that they thought was perfect for Martina McBride or Trisha Yearwood. They'd call me and say, "Hey we got this song. We need a key from you, because we're going to track it in the studio on Monday at ten A.M." Then I'd show up at three P.M. the same day and put my vocal on it. Then they'd mix it, give it to the publisher, who would then take it to Martina McBride's record company and play it for someone in the A&R (or Artists & Repertoire) department.

The record company guy might reject the song himself or send it to Martina's producer, who might reject it, or to Martina herself, who might reject it. Or Martina and the producer could really like it, but have no place on her current album for it. So, for that poor little song, there are a lot of hurdles to clear before it ever shows up on a CD or country radio.

This is all very serious business, because there is a lot of money—millions—in publishing a song that becomes a giant hit and maybe even a popular standard for years to come. Because of this, being a singer-songwriter can give you a lot more staying power in Nashville than just being a performer. It gives you at least two sources of income—publishing and recording.

Now back to my own demo work. It wasn't too long after I had Grace that I started getting an increasing number of calls to sing on demos. Sometimes I might be in a studio with John or another one of my cohorts recording a demo of their song, and someone at the studio would say, "Hey, you're good—let me jot your name down." It was a word-of-mouth business and like everything in Nashville, at first the calls were few and far between but then began to pick up. Pretty soon I was one of the primary "go-to" girls when it came to demo-singing. It was how I supported myself and the family before I finally got my own recording contract.

There were only a few female demo vocalists at that time who could sing well and give a certain song a certain style and passion that might appeal to a certain star. If you are a songwriter who's pitching a song to Trisha Yearwood, you want the demo to sound like Trisha Yearwood so that she can hear herself singing that song. If you sing on enough demos, you can learn a lot of different singing techniques. That was another part of my musical education before I landed a deal.

The way the demo recording business works, they pay you per song, which means, they pay you the same whether it takes you five minutes or five hours to get that song down right. I got good at doing a great demo quick. This really helps if you're trying to get back to your toddler or if you have that toddler right in the studio with you. It also means you can record more songs in a given day or week. And I did a hell of a lot. I bet there are probably three thousand songs sitting around on Music Row with my voice on them. For a while there, I was damn near the Queen of the Demos.

It's kind of funny, but now, years later, I can turn on the radio and hear a song that I originally recorded as a demo. I can even hear how the artist singing it borrowed some of the licks that I had come up with for the demo. It doesn't bother me now—it's all part of the process of getting a song demoed, sold, and recorded. God knows I've been influenced by singing styles and licks that I've heard over the years, from Tanya Tucker to Nancy Wilson.

And I would take my little Grace with me to every demo recording session I could. I would haul her from studio to studio in her little car-carrier seat. I called it her "pumpkin seat." I'd often put her in one of those glass-enclosed acoustical vocal booths that are completely soundproof. I'd close the door while I recorded a track so that she wouldn't ruin the take by crying or making a racket. She could see me through the glass and I could see her while I was singing. Soon Grace and I were doing five or six demo sessions a week. I wasn't getting rich but I was making a decent living and I was getting my name out there, not just as a demo singer, but as a singer, period.

Demo-singing was definitely a way in for me, along with the association with the talented people in the Muzik Mafia. Because of my spreading reputation in the world of demos, I had a chance to do a number of showcases for industry decision-makers. A formal showcase is different from the in-office kind of audition that I did for John Grady that landed me my first deal. A showcase is a stage performance for invited recording company A&R executives and managers and songwriters and anyone with any clout that you can get to come out on a Thursday night and hear you sing a set of songs. If you're going to throw a showcase, you have to spend some money, most likely money out of your own pocket. Even if your musician friends pitch in to help, there are unavoidable costs in mounting a public audition like that. Unfortunately none of the showcases that I sweated over, prepared for, and performed ever led to anything. I actually met my manager at a private party and got a contract in a sterile office at eight o'clock in the morning. Go figure.

From demo studios to riding with me on my tour bus to hanging out backstage at huge municipal arenas, Grace has grown up around musicians, stagehands, truck drivers, and a host of other people associated with a life in music. It is terribly painful to this day to have to tell her that Mommy has to go away for days or even weeks and do her work, leaving the one she loves most at home. It's not pleasant to get a phone call saying, "So, where are you tonight, Mommy? When will you be home? Will you be home soon? I got a lot of stuff to show you . . ."

Given the circumstances, much of this separation is unavoidable, but there are ways to minimize it and I'm trying to find every one in the book. It's imperative, for instance, that Grace has a good relationship with her father, which we've all tried to maintain. And, also, with all the traveling in our lives, it's important that Grace feels like she has a real home, with her own room, her own pets, her own friends, and a few loving relatives in shouting distance. I know the other way for a child to grow up—the way I grew up—and I don't want Grace's life to be that fragmented, full of stress and often lonely.

Even so, there have been times when she has rebelled against this back-and-forth separation. I remember one specific occasion after I had become "an overnight sensation" that brought this home in a big way. We were at home at the time and Grace was walking across the living room from her bedroom. One of my videos came on CMT, for probably the fiftieth time, and Grace stopped to catch it for a moment. Then she looked at me and her daddy, rolled her eyes, took a deep breath, and announced:

"I am so sick of Gretchen Wilson."

I knew exactly what she meant—she was sick of Gretchen Wilson the singer, the performer, the interviewee, the *business.* I remember at the time hoping I'd never, ever hear, "I'm sick of *Mommy.*" As long as it was "Gretchen Wilson," at least for the time being, that was fine. There are days where I get a little fed up with all this "Gretchen Wilson" craziness myself.

When Grace is on the road with me, she kind of takes over, creating her own little world in the backstage dressing room and making friends with anyone in sight. For instance, as we're doing this book, she is six and she is infatuated with the lead guitarist in my band, Dean Hall. She's crazy about Dean. She acts like a fourteen-year-old girl around him. She writes him little notes and stuffs them in the hole in his guitar. Dean saves them and when Grace comes with us on the road again, she'll ask, "Do you still have that note?" and he'll say, "Sure." It's their own little friendship game.

The advantage of all of this for Grace is that she meets and gets to know all kinds of people, often strange, one-of-a-kind people. The show business environment she is privy to is sure a lot different than growing up in the isolated world of Pocahontas, Illinois. There are strange people there, too, of course, just not as many, I guess.

Because she is around so many different people, she is not lacking in social skills. She is not the shy, retiring type. She loves to be the center of attention, especially on the road, and she loves the camaraderie of the band and crew. I like to say that she has never met a stranger. She loves everyone.

Typical of the way Grace encounters the world is the first time she met Fred Gill. Fred is a dwarf who is both an amazing entrepreneur—his ventures include the Funkey Monkey tavern in Seymour, Indiana—and an integral part of the Muzik Mafia community. His official title is "Ambassador of Attractions" for Big & Rich. He is all of three feet, two inches and a wonderful free spirit. We affectionately refer to him as "Two Foot Fred."

Well, the first time Grace met Fred, she was a little freaked out. She looked at me in a kind of scared way and said, "Mommy, why is he so little?"

I said, "I don't know, baby, he's a dwarf." Always tell your kid the truth, I strongly believe, even if it is at times a little confusing.

So Grace walked up to Fred, made a little small talk, and then just asked him straight out, "So, why are you so little?"

Without skipping a beat, Fred looked her in the eye and said, "'Cause that's the way God made me."

Grace came right back with, "Oh, okay. You want to see my new trick?"

It was that simple. Case closed. The innocence of a child can blow you away from time to time and point out how we adults can be so messed up when it comes to people who are different from us. My grandpa thought all Italians, not to mention every other ethnic group on earth, were not to be trusted. Thankfully, Grace, growing up in a world full of all kinds of strange and wonderful people, won't have the same blanket prejudices.

Grace has changed me in so many ways. Although I had drinking problems in the past, for instance, I don't think

I'll have another one as long as she is in my life. Since she arrived, I realized that I was no longer living just for myself and my own wants and needs. I was living for her, too. In the simplest of terms, it was not all about me anymore. This is a very good thing to remember when you get caught up in a star-making business where the person on the pedestal is often led into thinking that he or she is the center of the known universe. Grace walks into the room and that kind of egomania goes right out the window.

The bottom line is, Grace is my life and music is my talent and passion. I think music can be a wonderful, healing thing. It can change people's lives sometimes, and certainly change their mood or outlook during times of trouble and stress. And it is a wonderful thing to be able to stand on stage and do what I do for a living. But, having said that, the ultimate reality in my life is my daughter. That's who I really am. I'm a mom first, a singer second.

Through careful planning, keeping my priorities straight, and maybe a little luck, I've been able to stay close to my precious daughter and still be the "Gretchen Wilson" that sometimes irritates her. It is not always easy, especially right after my career took off like a shot, and I'm sure Grace still has some complaints at times about our unusual life together and apart. But, with the help of my extended family and the people I work with who understand how I feel about Grace, we've made it work pretty well up to now. I think I'm doing, and will continue to do, everything I can to see that my daughter can grow up with more advantages, and in a healthier environment, than I did. Just like my grandma, my mom, and me, she's a redneck woman, too, and will probably, sooner or later, show us just how far a redneck woman can go.

Having centered my personal life around Grace, the next big step in my career—meeting my managers—also involved children, ironically. Longtime music promoter and manager Marc Oswald, who was already handling the career of Big & Rich, held a kind of barbecue-pool party at his house in honor of a group of people in Nashville, including himself, who had adopted young orphans from Russia. John and Kenny were invited and brought me along. I didn't know Marc but I knew him by reputation. He had promoted massive country shows, produced a lot of network television, and knew his way around Nashville. John had been telling Marc about me and they both thought this was the perfect occasion to introduce me to a bunch of insiders, including legendary manager Dale Morris. Dale's clients include Alabama and Kenny Chesney. It was an honor just to meet him, let alone end up being represented by him.

So I went to Marc's party and kind of hid behind John and Kenny in a setting where I knew very few people. To quote Marc, "She hadn't been to too many pool parties, at least not where the pool was in the ground." Along with Big & Rich, I got up and sang a couple of songs. Even amidst all the kids and craziness of that party, I must have made an impression, because it wasn't too long before both Dale and Marc began to help guide my career. Today they

**My first photo
shoot in Illinois**
(© Marc Oswald)

**Me, and the Gibson
Chopper–first photo shoot**
(© Marc Oswald)

**My first photo
shoot in Illinios**
(© Marc Oswald)

Me, Hank, and Rock at the "Redneck Woman" video shoot
(© Marc Oswald)

Me and Vern at the "Redneck Woman" video shoot
(© Marc Oswald)

Chatting with Dale Morris before the show (© Marc Oswald)

"Redneck Woman" video shoot (© Marc Oswald)

Backstage with Kid Rock (© Marc Oswald)

"Save a Horse" video shoot (© Marc Oswald)

Me and Tony Bennett–Ireland
(© Marc Oswald)

Big O, me, and Ed Bradley–*60 Minutes* interview
(© Marc Oswald)

Super Bowl XXXIX
(© Marc Oswald)

"California Girls" video shoot
(from left, David Haskell, me,
Marc Oswald, and directors
Robert Deaton and George Flanigen)
(© Marc Oswald)

Vicky McGehee at the
"California Girls" video shoot
(© Marc Oswald)

Me, Candy Burton, and Vicky
McGehee at the "California
Girls" video shoot
(© Marc Oswald)

Grace on her horse, Doc
(© Gretchen Wilson)

Aunt Vickie Willis, farm manager, with Doc
(© Dennis Willis)

Cousin Matt Simmonds, director of maintenance
(© Dennis Willis)

**Uncle Vern Heuer,
farm groundskeeper**
(© Dennis Willis)

**Brother Josh and sis-in-law
Amy, merchandise**
(© Dennis Willis)

**Uncle Dennis Willis, special
projects coordinator**
(© Dennis Willis)

Me and Grace
(© Gretchen Wilson)

Me and Grace in Vegas
(© Gretchen Wilson)

Discovery Cove 2006
(© Gretchen Wilson)

"Redneck Woman" video still (© Sony BMG Music Entertainment)

"Here for the Party" video still (© Sony BMG Music Entertainment)

"When I Think About Cheatin'" video still (© Sony BMG Music Entertainment)

"All Jacked Up" video still (© Sony BMG Music Entertainment)

"Politically Uncorrect" **video still** (© Sony BMG Music Entertainment)

"California Girls" video still (© Sony BMG Music Entertainment)

GW and G-Dub
(© The White House Archive)

are my co-managers and are involved in every aspect of my professional life.

The big meeting at Sony with John Grady came about through the Sony A&R man at the time, Mark Wright. It was Mark's job to find "artists" and develop their "repertoire." I had met Mark at another failed audition at another label and though the label head politely ran me out of his office, Mark liked what I was up to. When he moved to Sony, he remembered my name. Through two local contacts, Cory Gierman of Muzik Mafia fame and Greg Perkins, a tavern owner and friend, I got a meeting coordinated by Mark Wright to go in and meet John Grady.

At the very last minute, not wanting to walk into the high-powered meeting all by myself, I called Dale Morris and asked if he would come with me and represent me as management. He said yes, I'm happy to report, and the rest, as they say, is history.

When I look back, I owe a lot of people a lifetime of gratitude for helping me get to that particular, life-changing, in-office showcase. I could say, for instance, that I got my record deal specifically because of Mark Wright. But that would leave out a roomful of people who got me to the place where Mark introduced me to John Grady. John Rich, Big Kenny, Sharon Vaughn, Cory Gierman, Greg Perkins, and a bunch of others had been setting up showcases for me and spreading my name around for a long time. So who got me my big break? I'd have to say, in all fairness, every last one of them.

CHAPTER

NOT BAD FOR A BARTENDER

Not bad for a bartender
Or an eighth grade education
Pretty good for a backwoods girl, who had to make it
*   on her own*
I'm on the stool side of the bar these days buying
*   everyone a round*
Ain't it funny how the tables turned
Not bad for a bartender

"Not Bad for a Bartender"

The night after the morning I sang in John Grady's office and he handed me the note that said "NOW," John Rich and I were out celebrating and we ended up in front of the Ryman Auditorium, the longtime spiritual home—almost the Vatican—of the Grand Ole Opry and, in a way, a shrine to all of country music, back to the days of the Carter Family and Jimmie Rodgers, "The Singing Brakeman." Standing in front of the Ryman is like standing in front of a Gothic cathedral. It seems ancient and sacred, and it's usually empty these days and kind of quiet and ghostly.

Anyway, just for the hell of it, John and I went around to the side and tried to open the door. To our surprise, it was unlocked. So I look at John and say, "So, you want to go in?" John immediately replies, "Let's go."

The place was totally empty. We look around and see nothing but this dark, all-wood theater converted from an actual church that was originally built in 1892. On the empty stage, though, we spot a guitar just sitting there. John picks up the guitar, strums a few chords, and begins a song so familiar to me that I just opened my mouth and start singing. The Patsy Cline classic, "Leavin' on Your Mind." It was a magical moment for me. Here I was, standing on the stage of the Ryman, just like Patsy, and singing a song I felt I was born to sing, just like Patsy. It was like Dorothy arriving at the gates of Oz after that long trek down the yellow brick road. I even repeat that image in the song "Not Bad for a Bartender":

> Swinging doors and cleaning floors is all I'd ever
>   known
> Then out of nowhere somehow I found my yellow
>   brick road

And now I was in Oz. As I was singing "Leavin' on Your Mind," a security guard showed up, ready to hustle us out of the building. Either out of politeness or because she liked the sound of my voice singing that familiar ballad, she let me finish the song. Then she tossed us out.

Later we went back to the Ryman, having gotten all the proper clearances, and filmed a fantasy version of that moment for the video for my song "When I Think About Cheatin'." We even added the exact date of that original "break-in"—August 27, 2003, 1:04 A.M. Like in the real story, John finds a door open and he and I mount the stage to do a song. This time it's my own "cheatin'" song, told from a woman's point of view and sung in front of an old-time Opry microphone. Both the stage and the audience are haunted with the ghostly presence of some of the great performers of the Opry. Through the magic of special effects, as I sing, I am surrounded by the likes of Conway Twitty, Roy Acuff, Little Jimmy Dickens, Hank Sr., Floyd Cramer, and of course, Patsy Cline. In the video, you can actually see them in the room. In reality, I just felt them, strongly.

Later, on my second CD, we introduce the song "One Bud Wiser," with another nod to the Opry. "Ladies and gentlemen," John Rich says in his best old-timey voice, "Welcome to the Grand Ole Opry here in Nashville, Tennessee. All the way from Pocahontas, Illinois, it's Gret-chen Wilson!" We thought it fit the song perfectly. "One Bud Wiser" sounds like a classic Opry tune, doesn't it?

I guess at the moment when John and I first got up on that empty Ryman stage and I sang "Leavin' on Your Mind," I felt in my heart that I had finally been invited to join those great country performers, at least for one record distributed by Sony. I had just made a long, strange journey from a Patsy

Cline song playing on my grandma's record player back in Greenville, Illinois, to a Patsy Cline song on the stage of the Grand Ole Opry. If I hadn't reached the top of the mountain, I was damn close.

Now, of course, all I had to do was to write, sing, and record a damn album, something I'd never done before. At that point, I hadn't written any of the songs that people now associate with me. I hadn't written or co-written "Redneck Woman," "Here for the Party," or all of the songs that were part of that first album. I guess it took actually signing that deal for me to say to myself, "Holy s**t, girl, this is it! You got to write those songs. You got to say what you want to say—and you've got to do it right now!"

I sat down to start writing and I wrote every single day for the next three months or so. I wrote lyrics the old-fashioned way—by hand. I'd be hauling Grace around with one arm and trying to scribble down a lyric going through my head with the other. I wrote with John, Vicky McGehee, Rivers Rutherford, George Teren, and Big Kenny—anyone who could help me put a part of me into a three-minute song. I think I wrote a hundred songs in that first month. Most of them are in a drawer someplace, but the ones that clicked, like "Redneck Woman," ended up on that first record. Out of those hundred-plus songs we cranked out in that very intense period, seven made it on that first album, which is not a bad batting average for a relative beginner songwriter like I was at the time.

From that first audition with John Grady, I wanted to make sure that everyone involved knew what they were getting when they signed me up. I didn't want to pretend to be one thing, then throw them off when a different musical persona suddenly appeared. Well, if they had any questions about that, they were answered when I went in to sing this little anthem we wrote called "Redneck Woman." I remember the very day I played it for a roomful of executives. They about fell out of their chairs. They were very divided—half of the record company was scared to death of the song and the other half knew it was a hit. Thank goodness the "hit" guys won out.

The people who had to go out and sell the song to radio stations were a little worried about the language. I cussed a lot in that song. In fact, we counted up the cuss words—I say "hell" twelve times and "damn" twice. Some people didn't think that was appropriate language for wholesome country radio. The theory among a lot of researchers and marketers, I guess, is that country radio is only listened to by middle-aged soccer moms, and those moms don't want to be driving the kids to practice in their minivan and hear lyrics like "Let me get a big 'Hell yeah!' from the redneck girls like me." My own view is that there are a lot of hardworking redneck women out there who get up at dawn, work a job all day, and then take the kids to soccer in a pickup. And the word "hell" would not be a shock to their ears. In the end, for those of you who think about these things, one "damn" got changed to "rip," but all the "hells" stayed.

I loved shooting the "Redneck Woman" video. I got to go muddin' in a four-wheeler in a riverbed and it gave me a chance to include my friends, from Big O to Kid Rock, and to meet a few idols at the same time.

I first met Kid Rock at a party at John Rich's house. It was John's birthday and he was anxious to use the occasion to play the demo for "Redneck Woman," which we had just cut. He played it and Kid Rock, among others, went nuts. I remember him calling his brother on the phone and saying, "Dude, you gotta hear this song. It's off the hook. I mean, it's like Loretta Lynn off the hook!"

So we got to know each other after that and I invited him to be in the video. I knew he was friends with Hank Williams, Jr., so I asked him if he could get Hank to do a bit in the video, too. He hesitated at first, then went after Hank. Hank, I'm happy to say, said yes.

In a trailer on the "Redneck Woman" film set was the first time I had ever met Hank Jr. and it was a little awkward. The inside of the trailer was part of the video and I decorated it with a lot of personal mementos. I brought in a deer head for the wall and placed the urns of my grandparents on top of the TV set. I just figured they should be there, just like I try to include them in every family get-together. That may seem a little country, but they are always in our hearts and the urns remind us of that at every turn.

So I walk into the trailer to say something to Hank Jr. and can't really think of a thing to say. I mean, what do you say to a legend like Bocephus? He was close to the TV, so what I finally said was, "Hey, be careful there. Don't bump that TV. That's my grandma and grandpa sitting up there."

He kind of looked at me, pulled his glasses down to the edge of his nose, then looked at the urns and then the pictures of Grandma and Grandpa I had placed beside the urns, then looked back at me and said, "By God, you are a redneck, ain't ya?"

And then we started talking. I guess the fact that I had brought my dead grandparents to the video shoot was enough for him. He knew at that moment that I was a real person.

If you know that video, you'll also know some of the other stars who dropped by that day. When I sing "I know all the words to every Tanya Tucker song," I wave to Tanya herself, sitting in the audience. Big & Rich are there, too, of course. To me it was like a marriage of the past and the present.

The idea was to release "Redneck Woman" as a single to radio stations, then follow that a few months later with the album *Here for the Party*. It is not uncommon in the country music business to have a single come out eight to ten weeks before the CD that includes that single. If the single hits, it builds demand for the album. That's a lot better marketing strategy than just putting out an album that no one's ever heard of.

So we released the single in December of 2003 in what is called a soft release. This means that a lot of radio stations got to hear it and hopefully begin playing and promoting it right after the holidays. The strategy seemed to work. According to Marc Oswald, we had so many radio stations putting that song out so fast that it was like a call to action. The phones started ringing off the walls at the stations, mostly from women, I'd guess, who instantly identified with the song. Then the video came out right on top of the airplay and only added to the buzz.

The whole thing was like a musical tidal wave. It came out of nowhere and just hit everywhere at once.

A lot of people have speculated on why this song got the huge, almost instantaneous reaction that it did. The song is unique, but it follows a country music tradition of sorts—a male tradition—that announces that it is just fine to be an unapologetic redneck, from Merle Haggard's classic anthem, "Okie from Muskogee" to David Allan Coe's "Longhaired Redneck." The difference is, I think, this is a redneck *woman* putting out this "Hell yeah!" point of view and singing directly from her own life and experience. Marc Oswald's theory is that through that song, I gave a new face, and a new attitude, to the lives of millions of silent, largely unknown women just like me. Women who also didn't feel like "the Barbie Doll type" and enjoyed buying things "on the Wal-Mart shelf half-price" were happy to hear someone sing about their lives. All I know is that when I say in concert, "Can I get a big 'hell yeah' from the redneck girls like me?" I hear a sea of female voices—and even a few male ones—yelling back at me.

To me, the song is an expression of pride. It takes the word "redneck," a slur word, and turns it on its head. Anybody who works hard, raises a family, lives modestly, or sends a son or daughter off to the military can find something to relate to in that song. The original "red neck" came from spending all day in a hot field behind a horse and plow. I never pushed a plow, but I know what spending twelve hours a day working behind a bar and pushing beer bottles feels like. And I could have been in New York working that bar as easily as in Pierron, Illinois. Or I could have been raising six kids in a trailer in Greenville. On one level, all people in these circumstances, man and woman, feel the same pride in our lives. Let me get a big "hell yeah!"

In the four months between the release of the single, "Redneck Woman," and the release of the album, everything changed. The single was number one on the country charts for six weeks. It had reached that top spot faster than any song in the history of country music. It was a rocket going straight up. A couple of months before nobody outside of Pocahontas, Illinois, and a few friends in Nashville knew who I was. They had never heard my name. Now, suddenly, on the basis of one song and a pending album release, everyone in the universe of country music knew my name. I don't think anybody is prepared for their life to be whipped around like that and begin to move at such lightning speed. I know I wasn't.

It was all mind-boggling. It was a shock to both my life and my lifestyle. And everyone else's around me. It took me at least a year to stop spinning. And it was full of irony. First of all, at the point when "Redneck Woman" was becoming a smash hit, I was broke. In fact, I was more broke, I think, than I'd ever been in my life. I was retired from both of my Nashville money-making enterprises, bartending and demo-singing. I mean, hell, I was now the artist other songwriters were making demos *for!* Unfortunately, royalties on records don't just come in a couple of days after people start buying the records. It takes a while, anywhere from nine months to a year or more, before they slip a royalty check under your door. With funds from a small signing bonus from the record company and an advance from my management company, I had been living and supporting Grace while I wrote and recorded the first CD. But at the time my career was taking off like a moon shot, I was cash-poor.

Plus, I was on the road promoting the record, constantly. I did, among other things, a nationwide radio tour. For four grueling weeks I had to go from radio station to radio station, playing a song or two right there in the studio and talking about myself. Sometimes the radio stop would be a redneck barbecue on the roof of the station with fifteen or twenty call-in winners and some overcooked ribs. Then you wipe your mouth and head to the next town and the next station.

This was not only physically hard but mentally hard as well. I was ripped away from my family, on a bus with a bunch of people I didn't know all that well, and I was being asked to do things I was in no way prepared for. They don't teach you how to be a public figure down at Big O's. The truth is, I was scared to death. Scared and exhausted. I was overworked and wasn't getting enough sleep. At the same time I was trying to adapt to a lifestyle that was new, unpredictable, and foreign to the way I had lived for the previous twenty-nine years.

I was prepared to get up on a stage or even in a radio station and sing, but I wasn't prepared for much else involved in being a "rising star." I wasn't prepared to be a friggin' model. I wasn't prepared for glossy photo shoots. I wasn't prepared for hair stylists and makeup artists hovering around and fooling with my look. For all I knew, by the time they were through, I'd look like a person I didn't really know. I might turn into a prettied-up fake version of myself.

But most of all, I think, I wasn't prepared for the media. I wasn't prepared to sit in that radio station or in front of a TV camera and answer any and all questions thrown at me. I was deathly afraid of sounding stupid or silly or to have nothing come out of my mouth. I wasn't a talker. I didn't have anything earth-shattering to say to the world. I was a singer, sure, but really I was just an ordinary person—a single mom with a three-year-old daughter and hopefully a good job I could continue. I didn't realize how much I'd have to share my personal life with curious reporters everywhere. I still had a bit of the hard shell that Big Kenny pointed out, and it made me very uptight and self-conscious to talk about myself like that.

I remember my very first "phoner," i.e., an on-the-air telephone interview with a radio station somewhere out there in America. I was sitting in my house and I called a Seattle radio station and talked to a DJ with a show called *Ichabod Crane in the Morning.* I was so scared that I could hardly breathe when I called in. I knew the show was live and any goofy thing I said would be instantly broadcast to all of Seattle.

Today people like Marc Oswald will tell you I handled it all like a pro—that I had a witty or punchy answer to every question thrown at me. But I can tell you, in all honesty, I didn't feel like a pro. I felt like a girl from Pocahontas, Illinois, who had suddenly been thrown into this fast-paced, think-on-your-feet-and-always-smile media circus. I guess, in my own mind, I was somewhere in that circus between the trained bear and the lady on the high wire.

Nowadays, all these media encounters no longer faze me. It's taken quite a while, but I'm really comfortable with them now. I just speak my mind. I may not say what you want me to say, but I'll answer your question in my own peculiar way. My nerves no longer get shaky when they turn that camera on and start peppering me with questions. The irony is, I do get a little nervous now before going out on stage to do my regular ninety-minute show, a show I've done hundreds of times. What if I forget a lyric? (It's happened.) What if I trip and fall? (It's happened.) I'm surrounded by a band of great musicians and a group of never-fail technicians, but I still get butterflies waiting backstage for my name to be called.

Starting out, I was relaxed on stage and nervous in media situations. Now it's just the reverse. Somewhere along the line, I made a complete one-eighty.

With regard to the media, I just realized one day that there was nothing to be uptight about. The only people who really care what I say or do are the people who are listening to me, and those are by and large people I know, understand, and feel comfortable around. Those are the people who like my music and come to my concerts. Whether they are sitting in a seat in Row 14 or sitting at home watching me on the tube, they are the same people. Why should I feel self-conscious around them? They are just like me, and vice versa. Nobody else really cares.

In the midst of all of the early craziness surrounding the release of "Redneck Woman," we decided to return to Pocahontas to do a photo shoot for the first album and also take documentary footage of the Big O world I had sprung from. We all piled in a bus—Marc Oswald, John Rich, songwriter Vicky McGehee, my makeup pal, Candy Burton, a still guy, a documentary crew, and a few other stragglers, and took off for Pokey. We did everything we set out to do in three days working seventeen- and eighteen-hour days. It was one of those trips that made me stop and wonder just what the hell I had gotten into.

I was not in the press much at that point, but everyone in that area knew who I was and had heard that I was coming back to town with some fancy-dan Nashville types. One of the things on the agenda was to shoot me performing in a local bar like Big O's. The real Big O's was gone by then but Hoosier Daddy's, Mark Obermark's other bar over in Carlisle, was the perfect setting for this honky-tonk performance. The place was a tight fit—you could almost touch the ceiling by stretching out your arm. The crowd was rowdy and the drinks were good, but the ventilation sucked. Although it was January outside, inside Hoosier Daddy's it was a hundred degrees and the smoke was so thick that you sometimes had trouble seeing the person you were talking to two feet away.

Marc loves to tell the story of John's particular entrance into the Hoosier Daddy's world. John, still in Nashville-land, had decided to wear one of his prize possessions—a full-length raccoon fur coat, the kind of coat you might see P. Diddy wearing to the Grammy Awards. John had probably picked it up at a yard sale or the Salvation Army for fifty bucks, but he loved that coat. I was nowhere around when John, in his fur coat and red cowboy hat, decided to make an entrance into Hoosier Daddy's. According to Marc, who was right behind him, the whole crowd just stopped and stared at him, like a Martian had just landed in their tavern. It was like one of those scenes from a movie where the music stops and everyone starts to get up, ready to attack. John and Marc were smart enough to get the hell out of there, high-tail it back to the bus, and lose the John Shaft apparel.

I remember what I wore that night—tight blue jeans and a pair of black leather boots that came up over my knees. Marc said the boots looked like something Wonder Woman would wear, but they felt right at home at Hoosier Daddy's and I had a great time performing in front of the people I had known all my life. Maybe some of their parents were there at the Hickory Daiquiri Dock when I thrilled them with my killer karaoke routine.

That trip was important for another reason. It reinforced in my mind what I knew best and what I should be writing songs about. I had already written a few songs like "Redneck Woman" that identified exactly who I was, but there were more to come. Back from that trip to Pokey, John and Vicky kind of looked and me and said, "Here's what you need to say. Hell, you're missing it because it's your life and it's boring to you, but this is what you are. This is who you are."

Vicky McGehee is the greatest writer on earth when it comes to titles. One of my all-time favorites—"When It Rains"—is on that first album. Well, as we talked about that visit to Illinois, it was Vicky who came up with the title "Pocahontas Proud," and we got right to it. After a kind of Waylon Jennings opening groove, the first line said it all: "I was raised in Pocahontas, Illinois." Following were straight-out autobiographical lines like . . . "At fifteen I was tending Big O's Bar, I'd sing till two AM for a half full tip jar . . ." It was a piece of the life portrait I was beginning to include in a lot of early songs. As John had said, I was singing about my rough spots and the audience that soon came to my concerts knew just exactly what I was talking about.

Like I said, I started writing songs like mad after the record deal happened. But all of those hundred or so songs I came up with in those early days were someone else's stories. They weren't mine. They were either generic country songs with no specific reference to one person's reality or they were songs that meant something to the writers I was working with. People can sit here all day and tell you that a hit song is one that rhymes correctly, or has an instant hook, or is radio-friendly, whatever that means. To me, a hit song is something complete different from that. It's a song that the audience believes.

The album *Here for the Party* soon followed on the heels of the single and things got even crazier. The album was number one on the country charts the day it came out and was certi-fied platinum by the end of the first week of its release. In a little office ceremony, John Grady handed me a gold record *and* a platinum record on the very same day. The publicity demands kept increasing and I was just trying to keep my balance and sanity on a day by day basis. Things got big fast. I was asked to perform at the Academy of Country Music Awards in Las Vegas. I was getting ready to make my Grand Ole Opry debut, this time for real. I started meeting people like Charlie Daniels, whom I had admired for a lifetime. I got to play before a hometown crowd of twenty thousand in St. Louis—it was just like playing for the forty-five people who knew me down at Big O's, only this time they brought all their in-laws and everyone from down at the welding factory. And I started showing up on programs like the *Today* show and *The Tonight Show.* I seemed to be everywhere at once.

The *Today* show, for instance, was the first national morn-ing show I'd ever done and only the second time I had been to New York. My very first trip to New York, only a short time before, was to do a showcase as a new artist on the label for Sony executives. I remember talking to Jeff Foxworthy on his radio show the minute I got to town. He immediately asked, as he always does, "Where are you and what are you wearing?"

"Well, Jeff," I said, "I'm in New York City laying on the bed in some fancy-schmancy hotel and I'm wearing sweat-pants and a T-shirt and tennis shoes and I can't find a cup of coffee that doesn't have cinnamon or something in it." He got a big laugh out of that—wide-eyed country girl in the Big, bad Apple.

For the *Today* show appearance, it was a really, really early call, and for a late-night bartender/singer like myself, it was not exactly the perfect time of day to be on stage yelling "Hell yeah!" I will never forget setting up for that performance. We were outside Rockefeller Center and when we did the sound check and quick rehearsal, it was five A.M. and still dark outside. There were only a few people in that predawn crowd and half of them were probably wondering who the hell I was. (There are hard-core country fans in New York, but there is little or no country radio or other widespread exposure.)

So, at five o'clock in the morning in the middle of a plaza in the middle of New York City, it was time for us to rev it up and kick ass. And that's just what we did. The response surprised the hell out of me. This growing crowd of people who looked nothing like my regular fans were starting to smile, whoop it up, and call out my name. For me, coming from a world light-years away from this ultra-urban backdrop, it was bizarre. It was one of the strangest stage experiences I've ever had.

On that same trip to New York, I did *Live with Regis and Kelly*. After my second album was released, I went back to Regis and Kelly. This time, backstage before my number, I happened to mention to Kelly that my Aunt Vickie always calls it *The Kelly and Regis Show*. Regis must have picked this up on Kelly's microphone or something, because when he said goodbye to me on the air, he ended with, "Hey, Gretchen, say hello to Aunt Vickie!" He busted me then and there. Nothing gets past an old pro like Regis Philbin.

A lot of numbers were being thrown around in those early weeks after the album came out. Apparently *Here for the Party* sold 800,000 CDs in less than a month. Experts were proclaiming that it was on its way to being the biggest selling debut album in the history of country music. I broke all the records, they said, even some of those set by Garth Brooks. Of course Carrie Underwood from *American Idol* came along and broke my records. But I had all the bragging rights there for about fifteen minutes.

It was hard to grasp the significance of all of these statistics piling up. I was thrilled that so many people liked the music and just happy to be out there singing. Singing, I knew how to do. Everything else was exhausting. It was a dizzying life of bus-plane-bus-plane-bus-bus-car-plane.

And then the awards started coming. The first statue of any kind I'd ever won was the first award I won at the Country Music Awards (the CMAs). It was the Horizon Award for Best New Performer. The live show was the first time I ever had to say something to an audience like that. It was also the first time I had ever sung in front of the whole country music industry.

The song I sang was the ballad "When I Think About Cheatin'." I was so scared, looking out at all those famous faces. I caught the eye of Alan Jackson, who was sitting in the first row. He had a friendly look so I focused on him throughout the whole performance. Every time I opened my eyes, I found Alan. My thinking was, "He looks like he's on my side." I'm sure others were, too, but I was too frightened to notice.

Then I had to get back on stage to accept the award and I don't remember anything I said except that I had been in the back of the same audience the year before and dreamed I could be up here, and here I was. The rest is a complete blank. It's a good thing that I didn't get into this business to talk, because I wouldn't have gotten very far.

My first big performing tour was opening for Brooks & Dunn. I was the opening act, the very first performer on stage. I got to play twenty-five minutes and since it was summer and outside, it was still daylight when I went on. There are usually three acts in a country concert like this. The opening act, in this case, me, gets to play with the sun often glaring right into their eyes. The second act—on this tour it was Montgomery Gentry—gets to play in part daylight and part darkness. Finally the headliner, Brooks & Dunn, the act that everyone paid to see, comes on when everything is just right—the sky is dark, the air is cool, and the crowd is ready to whoop and holler.

Despite the afternoon sun and heat, this was great fun because I shared the stage with some of the best performers in the business and their audience was probably a lot closer to me than those people on the streets of New York. Even before that tour, I got to stand on home plate at Busch Stadium in St. Louis and sing, on national TV, the national anthem at game four of the World Series. Having grown up only fifty miles away, I've been a huge Cardinals fan since I knew what a baseball game was. This was like another Pocahontas homecoming, in front of the whole world.

It was in the middle of the Brooks & Dunn summer tour that we had a ten-day window, ten days with no concerts scheduled. I was ready to go home for a decent spell and play in the backyard with Grace, but my management gurus had a different idea—a quick, round-the-world media tour to promote the album.

And I mean, around the whole world. In that ten-day period, we traveled 27,000 miles. The redneck woman went global.

It made good sense, of course. The record was breaking worldwide and the timing was right to put a face to the music from Australia to Sweden. We took off and literally circumnavigated the globe in ten days in July. We started in Australia and then flew around the world to London, Sweden, Norway, Germany, and a few points in between. I did only four live gigs, I think, in London. Everything else was radio, print, and TV. We did morning shows, late-night shows, variety shows, you name it. In a place called Ulladulla, Australia, we did a long-running variety show called *The AFL Footy Show*. "Footy" refers to Australian football, which was the launching pad for the show. I shared a dressing room in the back of a semi with a muscleman and a nine-year-old kid who dressed up like Gene Simmons of Kiss and lip-synched Kiss tunes on stage. It was fun, but it was nuts.

Marc Oswald claims that the only time I lost it through all these interviews and appearances in places I had never, ever been before was on one occasion in Germany. I was trying to call Grace across four or five time zones and the connection was less than perfect. I missed Grace terribly—this trip was the longest time we had ever been apart in our life. Anyway, in the face of my frustration in trying to talk to her, I broke down and cried. I regained my composure pretty quickly but, frankly, I'm not sure how. I was operating on some source of energy I didn't even know I had. This was it, I figured. This was the time to go all-out, and that's what I tried to do.

The fans in every one of those places were great. In Australia they seemed to know who I was. In England, at least my first trip there, the media people knew about me but most music listeners had never heard of me. I did have a little trouble with the food in most of those places—even Australian beef tasted a little funny to me. I was happy to see that you could find a McDonald's from Melbourne to Stockholm. We once made a fueling stop in Singapore that was just enough time for me to find a McDonald's, fill up a to-go bag, and get back on the plane. I'm sorry, I was still a country girl—I couldn't go to Sweden and eat something off the menu like salmon fetus. Marc claims I am capable of finding a McD anywhere in the world in under three minutes. A lot of the time, it was either that or starve.

The accents occasionally threw me off a little, too. Most people everywhere spoke English, but sometimes it was a fractured English. In Oslo, I remember, we were doing a morning radio show and the interviewer was a very nice Norwegian man with only a partial grasp of American English. It was a live show broadcasting all over Norway; the whole country was listening in. The interviewer was asking me about how I wrote my songs, and in the middle of the discussion he blurted out the following question: "When you write these songs, do you feel like you've touched yourself?"

I knew what he was getting at, but my mouth dropped. My comeback, as I recall, was something like "I don't think

I'm gonna answer that question." I had already been playing this media game for a while. With questions like that, you either think fast or sit there turning six shades of red.

Back from that trip, and at least partially recovered from the weird food and strange questions, I was asked to do a feature for *60 Minutes*. Ed Bradley came out, spent some time getting to know me, and then together we took a trip back to Pocahontas. Ed began the profile by listing all the great things that had happened up to that point—a number one album, my first awards from the Country Music Awards and the American Music Awards, the four Grammy nominations that I had just received, all in a pretty short period. Then he went right into the meaning of the song "Redneck Woman." My answer:

"I've never associated being a redneck with racism. . . . I think my grandpa was a little bit on that side, you know? I loved him just the same, but I had to tell people, he's just— and I hate to say this about him—but he's just ignorant."

I didn't pull any punches, either about Grandpa or a few other aspects of my life. I talked about drinking too much, but also noted that I never had any kind of drug problem. "I attribute that," I said, "to being witness to some of my mom's problems. There are times I remember having to go get her at the tavern. She wasn't capable of driving herself home. You know, for a kid who's . . . trying to get to bed for school the next morning, that made me mad. I mean, it really pissed me off."

I guess I was glad to get that off my chest, in front of fifteen million of my closest TV-watching friends.

Finally, after endless months of traveling and talking and singing and posing and packing and unpacking, I got a break. For a few great weeks, I got to spend all day every day with Grace. By that point I had gotten my first royalty check and could at least pay a few people back, if not buy a few things for myself. I remember going down and picking out a new truck. It was a GMC Sierra three-quarter-ton pickup with an extended cab and four-wheel-drive Duramax Diesel. A hit record, a beautiful daughter, a new truck—what more could a country girl ask for?

But the roller-coaster ride soon started up again. Between the performance dates and the personal appearances and the video shootings, I had a new album to put together. Again, working with John Rich, Vicky, and other great writers, we turned out some songs that I felt expanded on the personal, almost autobiographical, tone of the first album. The more I wrote, the more confident I was that if I just said what was on my mind and in my heart, I'd keep connecting to my listeners.

"Not Bad for a Bartender," for instance, came from a line John kept repeating every time we got an award or went to some fancy event. He'd look at me, smile, and say, "Hey, not bad for a bartender." That grew into a song that truly expresses my amazement at what had happened to me. When I sing, in reference to my fans, that "I can't believe how long they wait in the autograph line," that's the honest truth. I'm thrilled, of course, but also continually surprised. "Who are they waiting for? ME?"

Of course what was sometimes on my mind bothered a few other people, which we found out when that second CD came out.

Take the song "Skoal Ring," a simple little tune about a woman who loves men who chew tobacco. Now, to me, that's country to the bone. The song opens with:

Don't need no diamond ring
Don't want a bunch of bling bling
The only thing I really need
Is a man with a Skoal ring

What I'm talking about here—as I had to explain to a few Northerners like Matt Lauer on *Today*—is the ring mark that a can of Skoal tobacco leaves on the back pocket of your blue jeans. It's not hard to spot if you come from my part of the country. As we were writing the song, I came up with a line about the singer (me) being a Bandit Girl—one kind of Skoal—and the guy being a Long Cut Man—another kind of Skoal. John Rich almost fell over laughing. "What's so funny?" I asked.

"Gretchen," John said, "only you could think that people are different because they chew different flavors of Skoal. That's the most redneck thing I've ever heard in my life!"

And that little bit of redneck reality made it into the song:

I've always been a Bandit Girl and he's a Long
    Cut Man
Somehow we still get along with different colored cans

When that boy comes home from work smellin' like
    the farm
That berry blend on his lips still turns me on

When "Skoal Ring" hit the airwaves, there was some definite mumbling among the anti-smoking crowd. Some people thought I was promoting the use of smokeless tobacco among my fans, especially impressionable underage girls. The attorney general from the state of Tennessee wrote me a letter and asked me to stop showing a can of tobacco on stage while I was singing that song. The implication was that I was contributing to the delinquency—and ill health—of minors by singing the praises of an addictive drug, not to mention all the adults picking up a can on the way home from the concert.

I could see the point. Smokeless tobacco is far from harmless. Used in excess, it can damage teeth and gum lines and increase the risk of developing cancer of the oral cavity, pharynx, larynx, and esophagus. Just because you don't smoke it doesn't mean the same toxins don't find a way into your body.

But I wasn't trying to promote tobacco. I'd never dream of pushing alcohol or tobacco or anything like that onto a child. I have a child, you know, and I don't plan to encourage her to chew, smoke, or drink Jack Daniel's. This is a song that happens to feature a very common figure from real life—a good-looking, hardworking good ol' boy with a big ring mark on his faded back jeans pocket. He is of age to chew, as is the singer of the song. I guess I could have identified the same guy by his hat or his truck or the beer can in his hand, but I choose the ring on his pocket. I in no way meant to offend or upset anybody, but the song rings true to me and says something about the people I know and like. Because of that, I'll keep singing the song and hope that parents out there will teach their own kids about the dangers of smokeless tobacco.

Another song from that record that got people talking was the one I sang with Merle Haggard, "Politically Uncorrect." It was a Merle-type song—say what's on your mind. I liked it right away because if you listen closely, it's a song about the pride and dignity of common people. It's not about politics, as many people assume without hearing the lyrics. It's about the underdog and maybe because Merle sings on the cut and the fact we say "God" a time or two, some people have seen it as a kind of conservative anthem. It's not that at all. Politically, you can interpret the lyrics any way you please, but the only point I'm making when I sing it is, "Hey, see these people. Give them some respect. They're as real and as worthy of praise as all those Hollywood stars and media types who pop up on TV every day."

Singing alongside Merle Haggard is hard to put into words. Even today, when I listen to that recording and his voice comes on, I get goose bumps and the hair on my arm stands up. Merle is a legend—in some ways, the epitome of country music—but more importantly, Merle is a great, great singer and no less so today than thirty years ago. I know I'm not the only one who feels this way, but if you listen to a lot of country radio, it's like they've forgotten about people like Merle. And Charlie Daniels. And George Jones. George's last record is one of the best he's ever made. Same with Hag. People ask me all the time, "So, what's in your CD player right now?" And the answer is, "It's the old-timers, man, and they're making music better than ever and no one in commercial music seems to be paying attention."

I have become friends with and hope to write songs with a whole list of country legends, including Hag, Tom T. Hall, and Loretta Lynn. Loretta is as real as a member of my own family. She reminds me of both my grandma and my mom. She is like an instant mom to whoever she is talking to. And she'll tell you exactly what's on her mind.

At one CMT Awards ceremony, Martina McBride and I were set to give Loretta a special award called the Johnny Cash Visionary Award. We were standing offstage as they played clips of Loretta's incredible career. Loretta, of course, is not paying any attention to this. She's going, "Do I look fat in this dress? Martina, tell me the truth, does this look bad on me?" So the three of us started jabbering about anything and everything until someone said, "Loretta Lynn!" The curtain opened and Loretta the Star walked right out.

On another occasion, Kris Kristofferson gave me a ride in his limo one night in New York to the premiere of *Walk the Line.* A couple of months later he was putting together a charity album featuring various artists singing his songs and he asked me to record the song Johnny Cash made famous, "Sunday Morning Coming Down." I of course said yes, but it was a very tough song to sing and I wasn't sure I had done it justice. I don't think I have ever sung a song *that* heavy.

I may have been the only woman to try to master a Kris Kristofferson song since Janis Joplin recorded "Me and Bobby McGee," and I guess I pulled it off, at least according to Kris's wife. Soon after that session, she called me and said, "I've only seen those blue eyes cry a few times and he cried when he heard your recording of this." That, of course, made *me* cry.

Someone asked me why I connect so strongly to the older generation of artists like Merle, Loretta, and Kris, and I guess my answer is that, like them, I'm an old soul. I feel like they are an important part of my career and can help me move forward as a singer and songwriter. In turn, I think I may be part of their careers, too, in some way that reconnects them to my audience.

A quick comment about another song, "California Girls," on that second album. Now I have nothing against Hollywood celebrities, but boy, they seem to be taking over the world these days, and that doesn't leave much time or space for the rest of us. We're not all movie stars or even need to be. The song is a response to all of those prefect size-zero female images we're all assaulted with every time we turn on the TV or pick up *People*. When John and I were kicking around this idea, he asked what Hollywood celebrity I wouldn't want Grace to be like when she grows up, and out came Paris Hilton. I don't even know Paris Hilton, but she seems like one of those people who are just well known because everyone knows her. No offense, Ms. Hilton, and I'm sure you're not the airhead all those late-night comedians say you are, but most women could never come close to having your life. And that's a good thing. As I say in the song,

"Ain't you glad we ain't all California girls?" And California boys, too.

"California Girls" is a great example of how the people who come to my concerts affect my work. Most fans don't know it, but performers rely on them heavily for honest feedback. It's part of the back-and-forth relationship that helps people like me grow and change. Fans tell me by their reaction when I'm doing things right and when I'm not. I started playing "California Girls" in concert for a year before we decided to include it on an album. The reason it made it on that CD was because the fans put it there. Their response told me I was on to something.

One especially memorable song on *All Jacked Up* that I didn't write is "I Don't Feel Like Loving You Today." Grace helped me pick that one. We were riding together to the store one day and I popped in the demo to listen to it, and when it was over, Grace said, "Mommy, I really love that song." Since I loved it, too, it was a no-brainer. It is a timeless, indescribably beautiful song, and I am so fortunate that it came my way.

There's a "hidden" track on *All Jacked Up* that I'm especially proud of. It's not really hidden, it's just a final track that gets no mention in the album notes. It's a Billie Holiday song called "Good Morning, Heartache." What was I doing singing a Billie Holiday song, you might ask? It was something I wanted to do since I was a kid and first heard Billie Holiday sing in an old movie. There was so much passion and sorrow in her voice. Music, I realized very early in life, doesn't discriminate. We all feel the same.

So we decided to record the song in one take, with no mixing or redubbing afterward, just like Billie Holiday might have recorded it. And we did just like I said when I introduce the song on the album: "Four players, one microphone, one voice, one take." We all crowded around the one mike, the bow of the fiddle hit the opening note, and off we went. It was exhilarating. In fact, as I later told one reporter, it was one of the coolest experiences of my life.

That first rush of my career lasted a good eighteen months. A lot of the time, frankly, I didn't know what I was doing. Other people—my managers, PR people, record executives, and the like—were telling me what to do. I just woke up after three hours of sleep and did it. By the time I attended and performed at my second Country Music Awards ceremony and received my second award—the first was the Horizon Award and the second was Female Vocalist of the Year—I felt like I had become a much different person in some ways than the girl who had walked into John Grady's office with a slight chip on her shoulder. I was a touring pro, a media pro, and more confident than ever about my ability to write songs that were true to me.

I slowly began to see how the game was played and became more and more involved in the decisions that were determining my life. I became a better businesswoman and career strategist than I ever expected. If things go wrong from here on out, I can only blame myself.

That's the career side. In a lot of other ways, I was unchanged. Despite all the exciting, mind-bending things that had happened in those eighteen whirlwind months, I was still a singer second and a mother and family girl first.

It was time to get back to the farm, or as we soon came to call it, "Camp GW."

CAMP GW

Some people look down on me
But I don't give a rip
I'll stand barefooted in my own front yard
with a baby on my hip

"Redneck Woman"

If you were to ask me what was the biggest change that I experienced after that first flush of success, I'd have to say this: For the first time in my life, I could breathe. Like a lot of people, I had spent most of my life up to that point holding my breath, waiting for something awful to upset my life once again. Living with my mother and stepfather as a kid, you never knew what was going to happen next. I always felt I had to be on guard and prepared for every unpredictable event that might occur, from a vicious family argument to packing up in the middle of the night and moving to Little

Havana. And we all held our breath about money. There was never enough and a bill-collector or an irate client was liable to be pounding on the front door at any time.

The constant worry about money alone can smother you. It's all you can think about. It's every fight you have with your spouse; it's every thought that goes through your head. Every time you look at your child, you're tormented by the question, "How am I going to afford college?" It's at the root of every medical crisis, since you probably don't have any insurance. "How am I going to pay for this operation?" It's getting someone out of jail after a DUI or a fight down at the bar. I can tell you, for a good part of my life, a thousand and one money worries were choking the hell out of me. I think they choke a lot of people, certainly a lot of people where I come from.

It's a very good thing, being able to breathe freely. Now that I no longer had to worry about where the next rent payment was coming from, or what kind of bartending job I could find to make ends meet, I set out to build a home life in Nashville. I bought some land in the country about forty-five minutes from town. Charlie Daniels lives out in the same part of the country. Charlie is a well-known figure in these parts. In a little nearby town, Mount Juliet, he built and paid for a beautiful park for the community.

This God's little acre—or a few of them—is really what I've always dreamed of in my heart. I've always wanted to have a piece of land that was similar to the land my grandma and grandpa lived on while I was growing up. I don't have any raspberry or blackberry bushes—yet—but I have a whole lot more than they ever had. Compared to the flatland of Southern Illinois, this place is all rolling hills and green, lush foliage. I just wish my grandma was standing on the dock of my little fishing pond right now reeling in a catfish. I can see her pulling it out, walking over to the cleaning stand, gutting it, and getting it ready to fry up at the house tonight. She'd love every inch of this place. She'd think she was in heaven, which is exactly what I think, too.

The house is not all that big but it's plenty big enough for me and Grace. When asked about my dream house, I usually say that I never want a house bigger than I can clean myself. First of all, I enjoy cleaning—it's almost a form of meditation, and a great time to sing. I was cleaning the day Aunt Brenda heard me singing and got me my first karaoke gig. Secondly, I just don't like the idea of other people coming in and cleaning up after me. That's just not right. That's not the way I was raised. The family pitches in to help, but there's no one around the house asking me if they can refresh my drink.

Then I asked the people closest to me—my blood family—to come join me in Tennessee. First my mom moved out and we got her her own place down the road. Then my brother, Josh, and his wife, Amy, moved out and took over a very important part of my business—handling all the merchandise with my name on it. Josh had his own masonry business—a high-stress job—and Amy was bartending and going to college when I called them up and asked them to come down and help out. I wasn't sure they'd like it but they took to the road and to the job.

Merchandising is a big business—hats, jackets, T-shirts, tank tops, pictures, key chains, posters, the whole nine yards. Josh and Amy go on the road every time I go on the road and they do a terrific job of managing and marketing all of those goods. Like a few other moves I have made, I see involving Josh and Amy in my career as both a good business decision and a good family decision. They're always close by. Josh and I spend more time together than we have in years.

And they keep an eye on all the bootleggers palming off shoddy crap with my name on it. They'll scan the words "Redneck Revolution Tour"—the name of my current tour—on a thin T-shirt along with my face and hawk it for ten or fifteen bucks. People buy them not knowing the difference. When Josh and Amy catch them in the act, they'll often say they were "authorized by the organization." Josh and Amy come right back, "Well, that's funny, because we *are* the organization!"

Then my Uncle Vern came out and is now living in his own trailer on the property while his own separate house gets built. I like having Vern around for a lot of reasons. I'm a single mom living alone in the country and being within shouting distance of Vern makes me feel secure. Plus, Vern can fix, repair, grow, or kill damn near anything. He'll put together a homemade trap for the large, scary snapping turtles we have roaming around the pond, then fix up a batch of turtle soup for dinner. Since moving to the farm, we've been constantly working to improve it and make it a wonderful place to retreat to. That involves draining ponds, clearing brush, cutting trees, even reconfiguring the landscape—Vern's in the middle of all that.

Next came my Aunt Vickie and her current husband, Uncle Dennis. Both of them had good jobs back in the St. Louis area—she was a steel welder, as I said, and he was a mechanical engineer and did design work in the sheet metal industry—but I guess the attraction of moving to the country and being near their "favorite niece" was just too strong for them. I'm sure glad they did. Dennis stepped right in and took over the administration of my fan club, another big job. He also handles any and all special projects that might come up, like putting together the photos for this book or maybe shooting documentary footage when we are on the road. If we had titles, his would be Special Projects Coordinator.

Vickie is a godsend. She pretty much takes care of the farm, the horses, and oversees darn near everything else. Horses are a big part of the life out here and Vickie is the chief wrangler. When one of our colts, Bandit, was born, Vickie was the only one here to help with the birth. She waited near the mare barn for weeks until the colt came, then called in our neighbors to help her with the birth.

We now have nine horses on our little version of the Ponderosa. Five are geldings, two are colts, one is a mare, and one is a pony. If you're ever planning to buy a horse, especially a horse for your kid, don't buy a pony. They are without a doubt the meanest, most ornery, most worthless pieces of crap on the face of the earth. They'll chomp at you, kick at you, anything to drive you away. Ours just eats grass, keeps the mare company, and not much else. Of course no one told me about the personality of ponies before I decided to get my own.

Vickie and the others are riding the horses all the time, but because of those crazy couple of years traveling the world, I'm just getting the fever about now. It's probably been fifteen years since I rode on a regular basis and of course, after the first few outings, I was sleeping with a warming pad between my legs. We now have a professional trainer who works both with the horses and with us to do things the right way. He's not really a horse whisperer, though. He's more like a horse shouter.

Vickie loves working with the horses and overseeing the whole farm, as does her son, Matt, who also moved out from Illinois to help with the family enterprise. It's definitely a family affair—our own version of Walton Mountain—and it couldn't feel more right to me. None of these people have ever done what they are doing right now, but we were all raised to be able to do whatever it takes to get things done, and the various jobs just kind of fell into place. Some of my family needed a new start; some just needed a new challenge or a change of scenery. They all came down and found their niche.

In her job of dealing with contractors, road-pavers, horse people, and the like, Vickie claims the work atmosphere in Tennessee is a lot different than Southern Illinois. It's more "relaxed" here, meaning people often take longer and work slower, meaning we all have to adjust to a more leisurely pace. To me, that's a plus. I've been in a hurry my whole damn life. Taking things a little slower is good exercise for me.

There's a real advantage to working with your family, assuming you enjoy being together. As Matt has said, he can come out to the farm every day and every person he talks to he knows he can trust one hundred percent. And I feel the same way. I can call Vern, Matt, or Vickie with a problem and not have to deal with a stranger who may or may not be in the mood to rip me off.

Vern has another way of putting it. "Where we're from," he says, "there are a lot of deceiving sons of bitches. And that's all they do. They don't work. They just con you out of your money."

Now surrounded by my family, I sometimes wonder how any of us made it to this point. Alcohol, drugs, and a terrible marriage could have easily ruined my mom, but she's now in better shape than she's ever been. Vickie's had a hundred ups and downs. Given what he's gone through, Vern should probably be dead, but he's probably out fishing right now. For reasons I can't quite explain—maybe just pure stubbornness— we all survived. We are a clan of survivors.

Living out on that farm is like a vacation for me. After being on the road, coming home to people I love and trust and have known all my life is incredibly relaxing. Life on the road is manic and to keep your sanity, you have to decompress. The people on the farm don't move at my speed. I have to move at their speed and it's good for me. It helps me to slow down, breathe deeper, and enjoy all that God has given me, both family and animals.

Of course, my Illinois kin bring some of their old life with them, especially Vern. Last Fourth of July, for instance, Vern decided to throw a little party at a place a ways from the farm, out on Chicken Road, where he was living at the time. People drove in from Illinois, pitched tents, and started partying. It went on for three days and rained the whole time. Everybody started calling it "Vernstock." Even Big O showed up in his wheelchair and got stuck in the mud two or three times. A very good time was had by all, but no one died and everyone got back home safe, as far as I know.

I'm afraid another edition of Vernstock is coming to my farm this year and it has me a little worried. I got Vern to agree to invite only ten or so of his rowdy friends, keep them close to his trailer, and not let them scare the horses. Vern says they'll just get up at dawn, fish all day, drink a little at night, sit around a fire, and tell jokes. Hell, assuming things don't get out of hand on day one, I'll probably even join them.

Since I found the farm, it's been nothing but work-work-work-beer-work-work-beer-work. We're all building houses—I'm building a guesthouse for the next relative that might decide they want to live up here—putting up new fences, laying new water pipes, and fourteen other projects. I hope to have a few cattle someday, for no other reason than we can saddle up the horses and get a workout wrangling those cows. Whatever's going on, everyone's part of it. I wake up in the morning, stand on my porch, and watch Vern driving around on the tractor, cutting grass or clearing brush, and bitching at Matt. Or vice versa. Or watch Grace jumping up and down on her outdoor trampoline. Or walk down to the barn and see Vickie herding the colts into their exercise bin or turn and catch Josh reeling in a catfish at the pond, then toss him back to grow a little bigger. Another relaxing, balance-restoring day at Camp GW.

But that's just half my life these days. The other half is the road. I've said that I really miss the farm when I'm on the road and really miss the road when I'm on the farm. They both have their occasional rough spots, of course, but they both provide a unique kind of satisfaction for me. If home is Camp GW, then I guess you have to call life on the road Bus GW.

Right in front of my eighteen-stall horse barn sits my touring bus, ready to roll when David Haskell, my tour manager and all-around taskmaster, gives the order. My bus is a bit cramped on the highway, especially when Grace or someone else is traveling with me. Sometimes I'll invite another songwriter to ride with me so that we can use the isolation of the road to work. Then there's always my dog, Gibson, a black baby Lab who flops all over everything.

I love to take Grace with me but it's not always possible. I had special cabinets built to hold all of Grace's toys and stuffed animals and games and everything else a six-year-old wants to have on the road. The bus has slide-outs so it's a little more spacious for both of us when parked outside a venue in Omaha or Birmingham.

When it's time to leave, I hop on my bus with my driver and meet all the rest of the buses at a designated spot so that we all leave together. We leave as a family. We all drive together. We all run together.

In all, there are seven buses and seven semi-tractor-trailer trucks that haul us from concert to concert. There's a bus for the band guys, all seven of them; a bus for David and the rest of the production people like Candy, my hair and makeup artist, and Crystal Dishmon, the tour coordinator; a bus for a whole video crew that comes with me to every concert; and then buses for all the lighting and stage people, including a full pyrotechnics crew in charge of the fireworks that are a part of my stage act. The semis are stuffed full of all the equipment necessary to set up and get going before I walk on stage.

A brief word about the pyro—there's a lot of it. Someone recently told me we were carrying more pyro than Metallica. I don't really know if that's true, but I do know we're blowing up so much stuff on stage every night that it's unfathomable, but it's an essential and dynamic part of the show. I don't really think about it anymore. Unlike the days of homemade, do-it-yourself fireworks with Baywolfe, this nightly display of explosions is professionally tested, rigged, and controlled. Absolutely nothing is left to chance.

The reason I haul around all this stuff and employ all those people—something like forty or fifty—is because I'm now the headliner, and the headliner is usually responsible for all the staging and lights and sound for the concert. The current tour is called the Redneck Revolution Tour and includes Van Zant, led by brothers Donnie and Johnny Van Zant, and the youngster of the tour, a really great young singer-songwriter named Blaine Larsen.

Having the Van Zant brothers on stage with me every night is another sweet irony in my musical history. Donnie is synonymous with the group 38 Special, and Johnny still plays with Lynyrd Skynyrd. If my life were a TV movie, Lynyrd Skynyrd and 38 Special, among a few others, would be the soundtrack for at least the first twenty years. They were more than just music—to many of us, they were a lifestyle. The words they sang and their attitude and way of thinking were a way of looking at life for us. In many ways, that music kept us going.

The two opening acts bring their own musical equipment but they set up in front of my stage set and they depend on my people to supply all the production and marketing elements like lighting, sound, video playback, promotion, and ticket sales. It's a big responsibility, and since I'd only been recording and singing in concert situations for about two and a half years, it was something I had to learn fast.

After I toured with Brooks & Dunn and before I became the headliner, I spent almost a year as the second act on tour with Kenny Chesney. Watching Kenny and his people work is where I got my entire education about how to mount and run a large-scale concert performance. People like Brooks & Dunn and Kenny Chesney remain at the very top of country music because they turn out hit after hit and when you spend your hard-earned money to come see them in concert, you see a show you won't soon forget. I'm a little greener than those guys, but I'm trying to catch up fast.

Marc Oswald has said I went from third act on the bill to headliner probably faster than any artist in the history of country music. Something that usually takes a performer five to ten years to do, I did in less than two years. This year I will do something like eighty-five major shows along with all the TV performances and PR appearances that are scheduled. When you add it all up, I will probably be out of town a total of

250 days this year. The rest of the year I also need for writing and recording. And—most importantly—Mom days.

The only way I could possibly spend that much time on the road and carry the responsibility of headlining arenas and amphitheaters is to surround myself with people I like. And that starts with the touring band. It took me quite a while to find the musicians who both fit me and fit together in a cohesive kick-ass band. Without the chemistry we have found together, both on and off the stage, I'd probably be miserable, everyone around me would be miserable, and the music would no doubt suck.

Dean Hall is the bandleader and electric lead guitarist. He's hard to miss—he's built like a linebacker, plays like a Kentucky version of Jimi Hendrix, and he's got that hip all-bald look going for him. He's also the son of country music legend Tom T. Hall, but he doesn't go around advertising it. If someone gets real excited when he hears about his dad and blurts out something like, "You're that Hall!," he'll likely reply, as a joke, "Well, I'd hoped to get the last name of Twitty but they were all booked up at the time."

Georgia boy Gaylon Matthews plays steel guitar, besides being one of the funniest men alive. As I said, Bobby Rolens of Baywolfe fame plays second electric, mandolin, and whatever else we throw at him. Ron Gannaway, another hairless wonder, plays drums; Fiddlin' Danny Hochhalter, all the way from White Bear Lake, Minnesota, plays the fiddle; Brandon Fraley is at the piano; and last but not least, J-Lo, aka Jeff Lockerman, is our bass player.

In the middle of all of this is David Haskell. He's officially called the tour manager, but that doesn't even begin to describe what he does. He controls my life, really, or at least helps me control it. He and I are like a married couple without the sex. He handles all the details of getting from one gig to another, then takes over as the sound engineer for every live show. The man is awesome.

When we started our current tour, David designated separate dressing rooms for me and the band, which is how it is usually done. I told him I didn't want my own room. "How boring would life be for me," I said, "if I walked into my dressing room and was in there by myself all the time?" There is now just one big multi-purpose dressing room at every stop, full of people coming and going, changing clothes, taking showers, and so forth. I grew up with chaos all around me and it's comfortable to me. Nowadays it's more like controlled chaos, but still crazy and unpredictable.

So, backstage one night, with all the band guys sitting around before a show, David exited the bathroom designated for the females of the group. "Hey, Haskell," someone yelled, "that's the girls' bathroom!"

Everyone turned to me to see what I would say. I turned to David and blurted out, "Oh, I don't look at you as a man or a woman. You're just Haskell."

"You're just Haskell." It brought the house down, but it's true. David and I are very close and there is no weirdness of any kind between us. Otherwise, we wouldn't get along as well as we do and the whole show would suffer.

Whether I'm backstage with these guys, warming my voice up by harmonizing with them on an a cappella version of John Prine's beautiful ballad "Paradise" or on stage jumping around like rock stars, it's all about the music and not much else. Road families like ours play music—we don't much worry about record sales or marketing plans or winning awards or all the other business of show business. We don't feel competitive of other artists like Martina McBride when they have hit after hit. Personally, I think Martina is awesome and cheer every time she hits one out of the park. When we're on the road, we just want to do a great show for the audience who comes to see us so that they will come see us again someday and we can keep doing this until we drop.

It's a strange life led by almost everyone in the live entertainment business, and it demands getting used to. I eat breakfast on the road around three in the afternoon and am often up well past the end of the concert that night. If we have another concert the next day, we call that a "school night." Some crew guys have to get up the next morning at five A.M. to unload equipment, and everyone else falls in line behind them. On school nights, we keep the after-show partying to a minimum, but we're always up talking and playing for hours. When I think about it, I've never really had a day job, except maybe as a morning-shift waitress at Denny's when I was fifteen. I've been training for the night shift my whole life. Anything else would be abnormal.

On a nonschool night, on the other hand, all bets are off. Especially at the end of a long tour run, things can get crazy in totally unexpected ways. The whole crew is upward of forty-five people and we like to get together and act up. One New Year's Eve, for instance, a crowd gathered in my hotel room and before you could say, "Who wants to arm wrestle?," a major free-for-all broke out. It was a friendly free-for-all, of course, but we were lucky no one ended up in the hospital. The whole crowd became like gladiators—we went from arm wrestling to chicken wrestling to throwing each other in the pool to blindsiding whoever got in our path. We all became twelve-year-old heathen boys. Crystal Dishmon, one of the small band of chicks on our road crew, flat-out tackled me and bruised me up good for a week or two. It's pretty cool when you can do that to the boss and not get fired.

But that's after the show. The main focal point for everyone every night is the show itself. When I'm on stage, I often pretend that the audience is one big video camera. When you are on camera, the film is rolling and what you do is going to be recorded for all time. Given that, you are going to give that performance your one hundred percent, totally undivided attention. If you think of your audience in the same way—recording you in their memories forever—you're going to give them the same kind of focus and concentration, and probably offer up the best performance you had in you that night.

And I try not to think. When I break my musical concentration to think, it usually throws me off. And it doesn't take much—a bottle breaking near the stage is enough to freeze my brain. At a recent concert some fans threw a big banner on stage in the middle of a song. It probably said "Hell yeah!" or "Yee Haw!" I looked over at it, started to read it, and almost forgot the words of the song I was singing. I've never blanked on a lyric yet, but I know it's going to happen one night—something's going to break my concentration and I'll end up humming the chorus of "Redneck Woman."

Then there's the problem of staying on my feet. I wear real high-heeled stiletto shoes on stage and am generally quite comfortable in them. I thought, "Hell, I could run a marathon in these things." Then, one night at the House of Blues in Las Vegas, I tried something about as stupid as running a marathon in stilettos—I tried to jump over an amp and land on my feet, like some kind of whacked-out rock star. The stage was hardwood and when I came down after my daring leap, my stilettos slipped right out from underneath me and my butt hit that stage like a sack of cement.

It hurt like hell, needless to say, but what are you going to do? I jumped straight up, grabbed the mike, and began singing the opening to "Here for the Party": "Well, I'm an eight-ball shootin', *fallin' on my ass* son of a gun . . ."

I made a joke out of it and got through it. If someone comes up with a little tiny rubber tip that I can put on my stilettos to prevent such a pratfall from happening in the future, please let me know. Not that I'll be leaping over an amp anytime soon.

Between songs on stage, I observe the audience. It's really important to me to see who comes to my shows. According to Josh and Amy, it's mostly teenage girls who buy the merchandise out front, and I'm damn glad to see them. But I also look out and see a lot of young couples, old couples, and whole families out there. I love it when a middle-aged man holds up a handmade sign reading, "I'm a Redneck Woman, Too!"

I think perhaps the coolest sight of all is when I look down and see three generations of women who have come together to the show. There's Grandma sitting next to her thirty-something daughter sitting next to her teenage grand-daughter, all of them jamming to the music. They are all "redneck women," at least in spirit, and all see the show from a different point of view.

Grandma knows all about Patsy Cline or classic coun-try cheatin' songs, so when she hears "When I Think About Cheatin'" or "The Bed," she feels connected to a music she has loved for decades. The more rock-oriented material, with the flavoring of Led Zeppelin or Heart, is new to her, but her granddaughter is jumping up and down and singing along to the lyrics, so it must be okay. The granddaughter herself might be too young to remember Zeppelin, but she loves the energy of the music.

That's where Mom, the generation in the middle, comes in. She's about my age and she's heard it all. She was prob-ably raised like I was, hearing Tanya Tucker in one ear and Heart's "Barracuda" in the other. She's old enough to have been cheated on a time or two, but still young enough to hit a nightclub or tavern—or Gretchen Wilson concert—and get "all jacked up." In any case, they are, all three of them, having a female family outing, one night where they can for-get about the world.

Back home, "Gretchen Wilson" the performer turns back into Gretchen Wilson the private person, mom, and vacu- umer. Many people raise their eyebrows in disbelief when I say this, but I really do shop at Wal-Mart, Target, and the grocery store down the street. And I rarely get noticed or bothered. All I need to do is put on a pair of khaki pants, some flip-flops, an old hat, and sunglasses, and I'm just another shopper thumbing through the half-price T-shirts, looking for one that fits. It's what I did at fifteen and what I do today. It just seems like the normal, Illinois-country-girl thing to do.

Recently I hopped in my truck with a cooler in the back, heading to a local gas station to pick up sodas, beer, and ice. I got some money out of the ATM, like normal people, picked up my supplies, like normal people, and got carded on the beer, like I was a normal teenager trying to pull a fast one. I walked outside and a man with a sheriff's badge walked up to me. It kind of scared me for a moment. What did I do this time?

He was a heavy guy, chewing on a candy bar. He goes, "What are you doing?" I reply, "What do you mean?" He said, "So you just come out like that?" I said, "Well, yeah. It hasn't seemed to cause any problems so far." He goes, "All right then," and walks back to the sheriff's car where his boss has been eyeing me the whole time.

I thought for a minute there I was going to be arrested for being a celebrity and *not* being surrounded by obnoxious paparazzi and screaming fans. Which is exactly why I live in the country where even the people who recognize me don't make much of a fuss.

Wearing a baseball cap when I go out is pretty minor stuff compared to all that I have been blessed with. I have true riches—a beautiful, healthy little girl, a large, extended family to share my life with, and a career beyond my most outlandish dreams. There's no better way to illustrate this than something that happened last summer. Right after appearing at Radio City Music Hall in New York, a milestone in itself, I was asked to perform at a big fund-raiser in Washington, D.C. I was very excited—the president would be there and I might get to shake his hand. Other country stars probably know presidents on a first name basis, but not me. I was like a schoolkid on her first trip to our nation's capital. "This is cool," I said to myself.

As I thought about meeting the president, I thought about the incredible distance I had come—from a little country girl singing in Kmarts or her grandma's trailer in the backwoods of Illinois to dropping out of school, tending bar, and moving to Nashville, to overcoming all that rejection and frustration to finally land that first record deal, to this—performing before six thousand of the most powerful people in the world, including George W. Bush. What a long, strange trip it has been, I thought, and look how it turned out.

I know one thing for sure: It is impossible to express in words how grateful I am for the life I've been given.

So I sang a full fifty-minute concert set, beginning with "Here for the Party," for the black-tie audience gathered for this big event, called the President's Dinner. I was then escorted backstage to meet the president. He was in a little roped-off area smiling and making small talk with a line of VIPs. I can't remember what I said to him, but as I walked away after our brief but memorable encounter, Marc Oswald asked me what it was like. I guess I was a little overwhelmed by it all. The only thing I could think of was that the president, the busiest man in the Western World, does hand-shaking "meet-and-greets" just like I do. He just has a hell of a lot more hands to shake.

From now on, every time I say hello to a line of fans back-stage before a show, it'll remind me of that once-in-a-lifetime "meet-and-greet" in Washington. Like standing in the Ryman Auditorium that night and singing "Leavin' on Your Mind," this was another high-water mark in my life.

Oh, yeah. Do you know how much money they raised at that President's Dinner that night? Twenty-seven million dollars. I repeat, *twenty-seven* million.

27.

My lucky number strikes again.

CHAPTER

11

THIS IS WHAT I KNOW

When I did that Ed Bradley piece for *60 Minutes* at the end of the first year of becoming Gretchen Wilson the country singer, they used the following quote from me to end the whole segment:

"I'm just a simple, ordinary woman. And I think that's what I'm trying to say—that it's really cool to be that. I think that's a lot of the reason why people have really connected to me. I am just like them. The only difference between me and a lot of women that come to my shows is that I can sing. That's the only difference."

I made this point throughout this book, but this is really why I wanted to write it in the first place. I wanted to tell people, especially those who like my music and especially women, about where I come from and some of the simple truths I've learned along the way. I don't know all the answers, by a long shot—hell, I don't even know all the questions—but a few things I do know, things I have learned from the hardest teacher of all—real life.

195

For me, I had to drop out of high school, grow up fast, develop a bulletproof exterior, and get out of small-town Illinois to realize my dream of being a professional singer and songwriter. As I said before, if you want to do what I wanted to do, you come to Nashville. Chances are extremely slim that Nashville is going to come to you. But that was my choice, or my destiny, and I was only doing the best I could with what I was given. By doing so, that didn't magically solve all my problems. It doesn't put me on some higher plane. It surely doesn't make me any better than anyone else, or even any happier. It's just the path I took.

There are women I went to school with in Greenville who, as I write this, are on their third husband and fourth child and they're also working at a job that was available to them in that world—being a waitress at a diner, say, or a factory job near St. Louis, if they're lucky. For whatever reason, each one of them decided to stay put and embrace the life she leads. It's her destiny. Should we feel sorry for this hardworking woman? Hell, no. She is probably happier, or at least more content than millions of women in more prosperous circumstances. She doesn't sit around and compare herself to Paris Hilton or the ladies in *Vogue*; she just tries to live her life to the fullest.

She's got four great kids, she's finally found the right man, she's working a decent job, she's at home every night, and she's pretty damn pleased with things. And, in the end, that's all that's important. It doesn't matter that the family income is low and she's always looking for bargains at Wal-Mart. It doesn't matter that the best house she is ever going to buy is a mobile home—maybe a double-wide with some up-to-the-minute features. That double-wide will do just fine. It will provide all the creature comforts anyone could want.

The point is, she's doing the best she can with what life has given her. Just like my grandma, and my neighbor, Diane Jackson, and my mom and Aunt Vickie, and hell, me—we all do what we can, and we don't spend a lot of time bitching and moaning about the crappy cards we've been dealt. Grandma showed us the way. We just carry on and perhaps take a certain pride—and gain a certain strength—in toughing it out.

My whole life has been an education about toughing it out, an education learned for women who can survive and find their way in spite of a mountain of real-life obstacles. It's been my experience that these women think very little of themselves. They have been devalued by popular culture and in turn devalue themselves and their accomplishments. If one of these women makes the perfectly human mistake of comparing herself to the richer and more famous, her self-esteem goes straight down. She is surrounded by love and trust and yet is constantly told by newspapers and TV to see that as less important than wealth or notoriety or a perfect figure. Having grown up around some pretty untrustworthy people, I can tell you—trust is a much greater treasure than a vaultful of money.

The irony is, I'm sitting here on my Tennessee farm living the life that many of these women wish they had, and I'm sitting here thinking about how awesome *they* are. They are not frilly or girly-girly or particularly delicate—most would rather drink a beer and watch football than go to the spa—but I respect the hell out of them. I am here, in many ways, because of them and the inspiration they have given me.

I guess what I'm saying is, if you can see through all the BS about the fabled "good life," see real value in the life you now have, and don't feel like you're missing out on something, then to hell with everybody else and what they think and what the world thinks you are supposed to be doing. Do what you do. You go to bed with yourself and wake up with yourself, and you are the final judge of the life you live or want to live. It's an internal decision, not an external one. The size of your home or trailer has nothing to do with it.

Of course, we can all trip and fall and we can all learn from those missteps, as painful as that sometimes is. We all have to learn how not to buy our *own* BS, which can be damn hard to do. You have to be brutally honest with yourself. If you're happy, then be happy. If you're not happy, then maybe you should re-evaluate your life. Maybe you need to change.

No one, in other words, is stuck.

However many times you look around in fear or frustration and say to yourself, "God, I am stuck with this man or this job or this trouble-filled life," you really aren't. I've seen enough people in my life become un-stuck to know that it's possible. It took my mom fifteen years and fighting through some serious addictions to leave an abusive husband, but she did it. I've eaten peanut-butter-and-jelly sandwiches for weeks on end and lived in women's shelters with my mom and I'm here to tell you, no one is stuck anywhere. Realizing that is the first step to changing your life.

And it can be damn scary, I know. I watched my mom live in fear for all those years, both the fear of being with her husband and the fear of being without him. I've seen firsthand and secondhand and thirdhand how scared women can get when they make the leap from the known to the unknown.

John Rich has said that one of the things he likes about me is that I'm wide open to trying new things. I'm not afraid to step out into uncharted territory. I guess you could call that either foolhardy or daring. Whatever it is, my guess is that this risk-taking attitude came from being part of an unstable family and being constantly thrown into new situations every three months or so as a kid. South Miami was certainly uncharted territory for a country girl from Pocahontas, and if I hadn't stepped out into that world, I would have just holed up in my room, watched reruns of *All in the Family*, and wasted away. And if I hadn't put on that blue evening gown and sang that karaoke version of "Blue Kentucky Girl" at fifteen, I'd still be throwing up for an hour anytime anyone asked me to sing in public. Only by taking risks did I ever get anywhere.

I'm looking at uncharted territory right now. Another title for this chapter could have been "The Unwritten." I really don't know the next song that might come bubbling up from my brain or whether or not people will like it when they hear it. Songwriting will hopefully keep me in the game for a long time, in the same way it's kept Willie Nelson, Loretta Lynn, Merle Haggard, and a host of other great artists in the game. As long as you can keep expressing yourself in song, people will probably listen.

When you ask someone like Marc Oswald where I'll be in fifteen or twenty years, he'll say I'll be a multimedia artist, doing everything from making hit music to writing children's books. If you ask John Rich, he'll say I'll be wherever the hell I want to be. If you ask me the same question, my answer is, "Heck if I know." I will just keep pushing forward, try to keep my life in balance, and see what happens.

And if it all went away tomorrow, could I go back to tending bar, living in a trailer, and playing clubs and be happy? I think my bartending days are over, but I have nothing against trailers and I will always have music in my life in some form. Barring some crazy turn of events, I will always have another precious thing—the love and support of my family, the ones who knew me when, know me now, and will always know me, whatever is going on in my life.

No matter what happens, I will forever hear my grandma's voice telling me—take care of each other. And don't worry, Grandma, I won't let you down on this one.

YOU'VE GOT THE STORY, NOW CHECK OUT THE MUSIC

AVAILABLE ON CD AND DUALDISC

THE FULL-LENGTH DVD

PROOF THAT THE MUSIC DOESN'T STOP ONCE THE SHOW'S OVER